Jocasta Innes is perhaps best known for The Pauper's Cookbook. *She has worked as a features writer for the* Evening Standard *and as a translator of French and Spanish. Born in China and widely travelled, Jocasta Innes went to Cambridge University and now lives in Swanage with her novelist husband and their two children.*

CHRISTMAS DO-IT-YOURSELF

Jocasta Innes

SPHERE BOOKS LIMITED
30/32 Gray's Inn Road, London WC1X 8JL

First published in Great Britain by Sphere Books Ltd 1975

To Daisy

TRADE MARK

Set in Monotype Plantin

Printed in Great Britain by
Hazell Watson & Viney Ltd
Aylesbury, Bucks

Contents

Introduction

I am sure no one needs me to spell out the benefits of a do-it-yourself approach to Christmas. In the present economic climate, as the cliché runs, the high cost of this annual saturnalia, coupled with the thought of all the bills to come, must make parents everywhere come out in a psychosomatic rash round about the time of the first frost. The solution is to draw on your resourcefulness rather than your resources, in other words, do-it-yourself. Without going to the lengths of breeding one's own turkey, and brewing one's own liquor (though I'm all for that too) it is possible to slash the cost of Christmas at a stroke by making presents, cards, decorations in the peace of one's own home (let others tramp the cold, wet streets and elbow their way through crowded stores) from a variety of inexpensive materials. It's not only possible, and financially desirable, it's also entertaining, absorbing and thoroughly rewarding, as I hope this book will demonstrate.

First, I'd like to veto the notion that home-made articles need apologising for. This attitude is hopelessly out of date, and belongs to the Age of the Amateur when home-made suggested flaccid jumpers with pompoms at the neck, wee felt Scotties to pin to your lapel and sinister disembowelled dolls into which you inserted your carefully folded nightdress. Nowadays we say not home-made, but *hand*-made, and complacently await envious oohs and aahs. Not since Victorian times has there been such a fever of knotting and beading and patching; 'ethnic' shops stocked with the hand-made crafts of Peru, Japan, India, to name but a few, do a roaring trade; we scour street markets and jumble sales for hand-embroidered Victorian underwear, hand-beaded 20s tea gowns, and scream incredulously over the minute stitches in a friend's flea-market finery. Quite seriously, there couldn't be a better moment for do-it-yourselfishness—the hand-made look is fashionable and sought after, the shops are full of reasonably priced gadgets and materials to make your work go more quickly and easily, and there is even a virtuous satisfaction to be got from the thought that your activities are helping to re-cycle waste, check inflation and instil non-materialist values into your offspring.

To anyone new to the making game, though, the point I want to emphasise, because it hit me so forcibly while I was compiling material and trying out ideas for this book, is that making anything with your own hands is enormous fun. It doesn't matter whether you are designing a paper doll's dress, or knocking up a child-size corner shop, there's nothing quite like the moment when the thing begins to take shape and come to life in your hands, except perhaps the moment when you have dabbed on the last dot of paint or lick of varnish and can stand back and gloat over your achievement. The pleasure is catching too—I didn't have to pressurise anyone in my family to lend a hand, they were already itching to have a go. And the results were often remarkable. Some ideas misfired, or proved unworkable for one reason or another, but having compared the things we made with Christmas goods in the big London stores, I am convinced that the average, reasonably intelligent and handy individual can make things no whit inferior to the commercial offerings. And in some cases, because one is working for one's own satisfaction, in one's own time, the hand/home-made article definitely scores over the other: it is more lovingly made, carefully finished and imaginatively designed.

The great thing is to get started, which usually means coming across an idea that sparks off the urge to imitate or go one better, and this is where I hope this book will come in useful. Have you ever idly thought about gilding sea shells, or cutting stencils or printing with polystyrene tiles, or making straw stars to hang on the tree? Well, this book will tell you how. For the nostalgically minded there are instructions for making a replica of a 19th-century Noah's Ark, or painted papier-mâché tree ornaments in exuberant folk style, or versions of Early American chalk figures in—of all things—fire cement. Those with ethnic sympathies might like to try their hands at beading a Masai 'watch', or running up a child-size edition of an authentic Kurdish quilted caftan. While for the make-do-and-mend fanatics, not to mention the waste-not, want-not zealots—a growing body these—there are suggestions for re-cycling paint tins, string, odd gloves, empty bottles and a lot more into useful, thoroughly acceptable (and excellently cheap) Christmas presents. I have tried to avoid the crashingly familiar—candle making, routine tie-and-dye (there is one section on how to tie for squares-within-squares designs), folded paper angels with doily bibs. One idea I *have* expanded on, because it struck me that hard-pressed folk in the pre-Christmas flap period might find it useful, is presents so flat and small and light they can be pushed into an envelope and dropped in the nearest letter box. Specialist hobbies—knitting, crocheting—are so well catered for by the various magazines that I have only included a few mildly trendy ideas, like shawls, pull-on hats, soft pouchy bags. Food never goes out of fashion, and it occurred to Arabella Boxer and myself that a home-made Christmas hamper would be a graceful gesture from country dwellers to their urban friends. So Arabella has been collecting tempting recipes for *Christmas Food and Drink*, while I tried to think up various ways of making the different containers look more festive and alluring, plus a few familiar but unfailingly popular contributions from the garden like pot-pourri, lavender bottles. Last but not least—after all, it is for children that we stage annually this odd, beautiful, hopeful celebration of the birth of the Holy Babe, now almost engulfed by pagan accretions like Christmas trees, yule logs and mistletoe—there are many suggestions the children might like to follow up—presents to make for parents, relatives and friends, decorations to add to the general glitter and excitement. Sentiment is an adult foible hard to explain to the dispassionate young, but I would just like to stress the inexplicable and mysterious fact that Granny, Mum, Dad *et al* will be far more grateful for something made by your own little hands than for the most luscious box of chocolates your pocket-money can stretch to. Mind you, there is a limit. My eldest daughter is still pursued by the saga of the ingenious hand-trap she designed for me one Christmas, from a polystyrene ice-cream container held together by a deadly fringe of upholstery tacks and baited with such irresistible and useful items as packs of needles, spools of thread and—cunning thought—a tape measure.

No writer has celebrated Christmas with more gusto than Dickens, and nowhere more persuasively than in *The Christmas Carol* and the Cratchit family's threadbare but rollicking Christmas blow-out. What makes the Cratchits' Christmas feast so enviable, so convincing, it suddenly struck me on hearing it read on the radio for the umpteenth time, is that every member of the family, from dear Bob with his pushed-up cuffs tackling the goose, to the youngest Cratchits dusting the hot plates, is being a-tingle with anticipation, rushing about, taking part, being *involved*. That, surely, is the life blood of any family occasion.

Things to Collect

Anyone planning a DIY Christmas would be sensible to start collecting useful odds and ends some months ahead. Most of this material would normally be thrown away, so you can tell yourself you are doing your bit to avoid waste. And of course you will be saving yourself money as well as a lot of last minute flap and frenzy.

So reserve a couple of large cardboard boxes and into them put any or all of the following:

Bits of cardboard: shirtboards, light cardboard boxes, offcuts of mounting board, backs of writing pads, etc.

Shiny stuff: foil, chocolate and sweet wrappings (smooth these out first), scraps of kitchen foil, broken tinsel balls from last Christmas.

Pretty papers: odd bits of attractive wrapping paper, coloured tissues, coloured drawing paper.

Fabric scraps: keep any pretty printed or plain scraps of fabric from dressmaking, bits of coloured felt, leather, odd gloves.

Wood, chipboard, hardboard, etc.: if there is a carpenter in the family this should not be a problem, as he will probably hoard odd pieces anyway.

Containers: cottage cheese and yoghourt cartons are invaluable for mixing paints, storing paste and glue, holding paint water. Also odd tins, jam jars, with their lids.

Nearer the date begin stocking up with some of the tools, adhesives and materials you will be needing. The following list includes most of the basic equipment required for ideas in this book. Some particular projects will call for more specialised tools, etc. and these will be listed in the appropriate section.

Sharp scissors, large and smaller.

Stanley knife and supply of new blades.

Adhesives: decorators' size, wallpaper paste, Araldite, an impact adhesive like Bostik or Evostik, woodworkers' PVA adhesive—useful for sticking foil as well as wood.

Gummed brown strip paper, sellotape, coloured foil sticky tape.

A selection of paints (undercoat, enamels, artists' acrylics, varnishes), brushes and appropriate cleaners, meths, turps. Rulers, compasses, T-square, protractor, mapping pens, felt pens, pencils—no problem if there is a schoolchild in the house.

Glitter dust, sequins, decorative strings, ribbons, scraps of lace, feathers, etc.

Eyelets in various sizes.

Rags for wiping things down.

Make Your Own Christmas Cards

I hope escalating postage rates don't put paid to the pleasant custom of exchanging greetings cards at Christmas. The run-up to 25 December wouldn't be the same without a new batch of cards to exclaim over every morning. One way round rising postage costs, as people are discovering, is to save money on the cards by making them at home. The results may not be artistically brilliant, but who cares about that? They are personal in a way no shop-bought cards could ever be, and that's the whole point of the exercise.

You can't draw for toffee? Well, consult the rest of the family, not forgetting the youngest, who might with a little coaxing dash off a spirited child's eye view of Santa Claus squeezing down the chimney. Print it up in one of the ways suggested below, using suitably zany colours, and you will have a card likely to appeal to grandparents and relatives and amuse your friends.

Alternatively, try collages, potato prints, jokey variations on the family snap theme. Lino print some sort of family emblem on plain white invitation cards (you don't have to draw like Rembrandt to produce a recognisable plum pudding, or a pair of crossed tennis rackets), or tile print (using polystyrene tiles) in white on colour for traditional snow scenes. Instructions for these and more besides can be found below. Whatever type of card you settle for, it is a good idea to start working on them well ahead of the Christmas rush. Rope the whole family in on the making too, they may grumble at first but they'll soon get interested, and with a repetitive job like this many hands do make light work.

Polystyrene Tile Prints

Polystyrene tiles, obtainable very cheaply from decorators' shops, can be used effectively for printing Christmas scenes, especially snow scenes, in white on coloured card or paper. Compared with lino cuts, which involve painstaking gouging and scraping, preparing a tile for printing is a cinch. They are easy to write on too, so incorporate Christmas greetings (written backwards) into your design to save time.

Materials

Polystyrene tiles, corks, darning needles, nails, broad pen nibs, a candle, coloured paper or card, white or coloured printers' inks, a small sheet of glass, rubber roller as sold for lino printing.

To Make

The polystyrene surface is inscribed with heated tools—needles, nibs, etc.—which slice through the surface as easily as a knife through soft butter. Experiment on a spare tile first, before working out your design, to get an idea of the possibilities of the tile method and the range of effects you can obtain with different implements. Stick the needles, nails, etc., into corks and heat them in a candle flame—they don't have to be red hot, just hot. The point to keep in mind is that the tiles will give what you might call a negative print, i.e. the areas that will take up the ink and print it will be the ones you *haven't* burnt away with your tools. The coloured paper or card you print on will show up your burnt away design. Thus, for a traditional red-clad Santa alighting on a snow-covered roof, you would burn away Santa's figure, and odd outlines, and print in white on red paper. If that sounds complicated, try it, and you will see what I mean. It is possible to reverse this process, burning away the background and leaving your outlines in relief to pick up the ink, but the spongy texture of the tiles makes it difficult to get a sharp print this way. To ink the tile: squeeze a little printers' ink on to a sheet of glass, and run the roller backwards and forwards until it is evenly coated. Then roll firmly over the prepared tile. Print by pressing down firmly with both hands on paper or card, inked side down, of course. Lift off quickly with both hands to avoid smudging. Leave the prints to dry overnight.

When you have the hang of tile printing, you might like to try more ambitious effects, using two or three colours, either superimposed or in separate blocks of colour. Don't be afraid to experiment—the tiles are so cheap and incising designs is so rapid, that it really pays off to spend an hour or so trying different effects. When printing in more than one colour, cut each tile to the same shape and size before doing the designs, so that there is no problem getting the colours where you want them as you print.

If pictures are beyond your scope, settle for a Christmassy pattern instead—like the greetings tree shown, which neatly deals with symbol and message in one operation. There is one snag to this delightfully simple idea, which is that lettering must be written backwards on the tile to print off the

Greetings tree printed with tile method

right way round. The easiest way to do this is to print the tree shape carefully the size you want it, on fine paper using Indian ink (rough it out in pencil first). Turning the paper over will give you the mirror image. Now trace this off through a sheet of carbon paper on to a polystyrene tile, using a medium sharp pencil point, or fine felt pen. Then go over the mirror writing with a hot needle. This may seem a lot of trouble, but think how many prints you can make from one finished tile!

Warning Don't let children work unsupervised with polystyrene tiles because they flare up rapidly if exposed to a naked candle flame.

Open the Door . . .

Family snaps are great for close friends and relations who will get lots of conversational mileage from them—'My, hasn't little Tracy shot up . . . I remember when she was just knee-high to a grasshopper.' As a change from the usual commercial card-cum-frame, why not develop the peek-a-boo notion so successfully used in Advent calendars, and conceal your smiling faces behind lift-up flaps. Fun to make, and amusing to get. (See illustrations for ideas on designs.) The house—it could be a coloured sketch of your own home—might conceal a small close-up of each member of the family behind each window, and a tightly packed family group waiting behind the front door. I suggest you draw and paint the cover designs by hand, since you will only be sending a few of these cards. Draw and paint the house, or tree, or whatever design you fancy, on thin card or good quality paper and cut round the flaps neatly with a sharp knife blade—not right the way round, of course, or they will drop off. Then lay the cover design on another piece of card or paper the same size and mark

Family snap Christmas card – house with lift-up flap windows and door

the positions for the snaps. Paste these in place, using Polycell. Then paste the cover card over the top. When the paste has dried, leave the whole caboodle under a pile of heavy books to press it flat. (If you weight it *before* the paste has dried the recipients will never discover what lies behind the firmly stuck down flaps.)

Potato Prints

Potato prints are childishly simple to do, but they can look very effective if you stick to simple shapes and print them in two or three harmonising colours. They are best printed in light colours on a dark paper or card. Try stars, large and small, printed in yellow, brown and white on dark green. Or angels in red, pink and white on brown or purple.

Select large potatoes and cut across at widest point. Wipe starch off the cut face. Draw out design with felt pen and cut round the outline vertically to a depth of about $\frac{1}{4}$ inch. Then cut away all the rest of the potato surface, so that the design is left in relief. Wipe again before printing. To print, mix up poster colours on a flat plate or saucer. Dip the potato design into the paint, make sure it is well covered, then press on to the card or paper.

Mini Lino Cuts

Making lino cuts, as I have already indicated, is a somewhat laborious and painstaking business, over a large surface that is. Making a mini lino cut doesn't take long because there is less background to cut away. Small lino cut designs printed on plain white cards (from stationers) make stylish Christmas cards. (See illustration.) This one, admittedly, is by an artist friend, but it gives an idea of the decorative potential. If your drawing ability won't reach to an original design, find one to copy—old books often have attractive decorative motifs at the end of chapters which would reproduce in lino cut. Old cook books are a rich source of festive-looking pies and puddings (you can add a sprig of holly) not to mention ornamental platters of fruit. Not strictly Christmassy, but pictures of food are always cheering. Look for bold, simple designs without too much fine shading and

Lino cut Christmas card

detail as these will be easiest to reproduce in lino terms. Print in black, dark red or brown, for the most stylish effect.

Materials

Small blocks of mounted lino, sharp penknife, U-shaped gouge for cutting and clearing away the background, rubber roller, printing inks in black, brown, red, small sheet of glass, white cards. All these materials can be bought from art shops.

To Make

The easiest way to transfer a design to a lino block is to paint the block white, then trace the design onto it through a sheet of carbon paper. Use white poster paint, which can be washed off later, to paint the block. Cut round the design outlines with a sharp knife, making a shallow ($\frac{1}{8}$ inch) V-shaped groove right round. When cutting curves, move the lino block rather than the tool. The cleaner and smoother your cutting, the better the final result. Half tones—shading, stippling, cross hatching—can be reproduced by fine criss-cross cutting, pecking out tiny shreds of lino. But don't expect to get detail as fine as on an engraving. When you have finished cutting the outline, begin clearing away the background using the gouge to a depth of at least $\frac{1}{8}$ inch. If you want to work a message into the design, remember that the lettering must be reversed, as in mirror writing. You can cheat by using reverse Letraset for the lettering. Transfer it directly to the block and cut round as before.

To Print

The technique is the same as for tile printing, except that greater pressure on the block yields a sharper print. Some people stand on the lino blocks for a few seconds, but do this with care as you could smudge the print. Re-ink the block between each print. You may need to wipe it down from time to time to prevent uneven colour build-up.

If a monochrome card seems dreary, you can always add one small colour accent—holly berries, the date—by hand afterwards. Wait till the print is quite dry first.

Collage

The technique of pasting printed and plain paper cut-outs and scraps together to make up a picture is so well known, and popular, that I won't go on about it here. I would just like to remind you that it is an excellent technique for Christmas cards, and you can get very interesting and flashy effects with a little imagination and no artistic ability, strictly speaking. Clever teenagers with a surrealist turn of mind are particularly adept at collage. The snag with the collage, of course, is that it is a one-off technique—each one is different and must be done separately. Use printed material of every possible sort—black and white photos, old Christmas cards, magazine cut-outs, and mix them freely, letting your imagination run wild. A trendy card I received last year with a 40s-type pin-up stepping out of a pair of giant lipsticked lips, with HI! printed above, suggests the type of visual joke that works well in collage terms. A newsprint Christmas tree shape hung with tiny coloured cut-outs—cars, girls, diamonds, etc.—would be a more orthodox approach to the subject.

Cut Paper, String, etc.

Children's cut paper kits, in lots of bright shiny colours, are useful for making up cards at the last minute. They are self-adhesive, which saves time. Use dark paper or card for the background—black looks good, if you don't think it unsuitable—and make up simple folk patterns with the cut shapes.

Another last-minute recourse is string, looped into Christmassy shapes and stuck down with size to dark, matt paper. Press under a weight when dry.

Wrapping it up

When it comes to wrapping up Christmas presents I am torn between the wish to make something shiny and exciting of my parcels and a reluctance to spend pounds on Christmas wrapping paper, shiny tape, ribbon and all the other etceteras. It is possible to do up your gifts in style, cheaply, but you will need to plan ahead and forego the conventional Santa, holly and tinsel approach for something more offbeat. That shouldn't be such a sacrifice—most of the Christmassy wrapping papers and trimmings available in your local store are poorly designed and unimaginative.

The best buy in conventional wrapping papers is white tissue paper, which comes in packs of fair-sized sheets. Try tying up white tissue parcels in red string, adding shiny stick-on stars for sparkle. You can make stars from gold and silver milk bottle tops, stuck on with Copydex or PVA adhesive. Coloured tissue costs a little more, and is harder to track down unless you live in the London area, but a parcel wrapped in a coloured tissue with matching ribbon or sticky tape always looks glamorous. Standard commercial wrapping paper is worth investigating. It comes in a good blue as well as the usual brown. Ring round local paper and board merchants (Yellow Pages) to see if anyone will let you have small quantities of the stuff. Alternatively, arrange with friends to share the cost of a whole roll, which would provide all of you with yards and yards of paper for a pound or so. Blue paper looks smart tied with bright yellow string stuck down with red sealing wax. Ordinary brown paper can be jazzed up with large shiny spots (milk bottle tops again) here and there. Or go for quiet chic with a stencilled motif (see illustrations) in dark brown or purple, with matching ribbon or shiny sticky tape. White shelf paper, in rolls from DIY and wallpaper shops, is about the cheapest you can buy, and it can be smartened up with bright stencils and coloured string and sealing wax. Use acrylic paints for stencils, as they dry so quickly, and use them quite thick for clear-cut stencils which will not pucker the paper too much. The best brush for stencilling is a thick, quite stiff one. Make your own from an old shaving brush. Gold spray paint (art shops, stationers) makes a very effective stencil against a dark paper, but be careful to mask off the surrounding area when spraying. Alternatively, skip the stencil and just give the parcel a short burst of gold in any pattern you fancy for an instant touch of glamour. A piece of chicken wire laid over the paper, and sprayed through gives a pretty lozenge pattern. (Don't be too lavish with the gold spray, however, as it could work out expensive.)

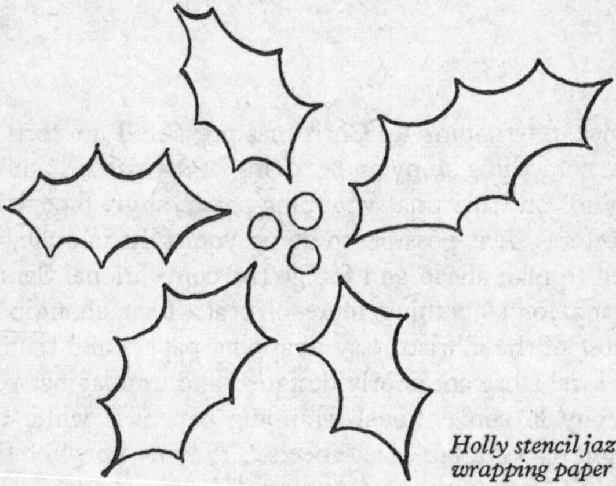

Holly stencil jazzes up plain wrapping paper

Etceteras

Plain white self-adhesive labels (stationers stock these in packs, books and rolls) suit the tailored type of parcel done up with string and sealing wax. Brighten them up if you want to by drawing a sprig of holly with a felt pen, or simply a few red lines round the edge. Make your own tie-on labels from plain white card cut round with a sharp knife and tied on with red string. Punch holes for the string with a punching tool—a punch for leather, paper, etc. with adjustable punches is a good investment for anyone planning a DIY Christmas (craft shops).

The Tree and Tree Decorations

The Christmas tree in all its shimmering splendour, laden with fantastic glittering fruit, is a sight to reduce small children to speechless awe and make even hardboiled elders catch their breath. It is magic, a vision.

Successful magic takes thought, skill and imagination. It seems to me that we have all got into something of a decorative rut with our Christmas trees these past years. Shiny baubles, tinsel swags and a string of coloured lights are undeniably pretty but a tree needs more than that to be memorable. The best trees I have seen were all unique in some way. There was one, very grand, decorated with heirlooms, strange carved and painted wooden figures and Bohemian blown glass ornaments as fragile as bubbles. In complete contrast I remember a midget tree an American girl had contrived for her baby son with great skill and imagination and almost no money, using homely materials like string, coloured paper and odd earrings. Another was a toy tree which might have come straight out of a Victorian sampler, and the most glamorous, an outdoor tree, white as hoarfrost, strung with nothing but silver baubles. Indoors it might have been a bit showy, but standing under a spotlight in a dark garden it looked superb.

The secret of a superlative tree, as with a superlative Chinese meal, is variety and contrast: the decorations should balance shiny surfaces against rough ones, lacy shapes against solid ones, bright patterns against plain colours, sophisticated shapes—peacocks, butterflies—against homely ones—apples, peppermint canes. These need not be expensive if you start from last year's collection of glitter and baubles, and make all the rest yourself. The next few pages are entirely devoted to tree ornaments to make at home, mostly from the cheapest materials—tins, papier-mâché pulp, string, paper and paint. It's a good idea to have a large box in which you keep any bits and pieces with decorative possibilities—scraps of felt, ribbon, chocolate papers, shiny buttons, beads, frilly paper napkins, lacy plastic mats, and broken earrings. You will also need various adhesives, cards of fine wire, varnish, brushes, cardboard. Some things like cotton balls and the proper shiny straw for stars must be obtained from craft shops (see Suppliers' Index). I have included some quickie ideas because we can't all be far-sighted and methodical, especially around Christmas time, but, ideally, making decorations is a pleasant, leisurely way to occupy the odd long winter evening, starting some time around late October.

Finally, because it is so rare these days to find a really bushy, well-shaped tree on sale at a reasonable price—no wonder so many people give up and go plastic—I have included some cheap, old-fashioned tips for making the most of a raggedly shaped or yellowing tuft of evergreen.

Papier-mâché and Paint

Painted papier-mâché makes pretty and original Christmas tree ornaments, and some of the cheapest. Little shiny red apples, angels, bells, hearts decorated with folk patterns, birds with feather tails are just a few of the shapes possible, and they look gay and charming. Making them is not something to embark on at the last minute, because to get a really good finish involves a lot of separate processes best spread out over a week or so. None of these processes—except perhaps the initial newspaper tearing—takes very long, but they should be approached in a leisurely spirit. Get the family to help with the paper shredding. Wait till they are all gathered in front of the telly, then produce a bucket and a couple of sheets of newspaper all round and tell them to get cracking.

Materials

Newspaper, plain flour, powdered alum, florists' wire, Polyfilla or Wallart, plain white undercoat, acrylic or poster paints, varnish or clear enamel. You will need a large metal bucket or outsize saucepan too, and an asbestos sheet is handy.

To Make

There are two ways of modelling with papier-mâché. You can build up shapes with layers of pasted paper, or make a sticky paper mash which can be worked like plasticine. I used the mash for these ornaments because it lends itself to small three dimensional shapes, and is quicker to work once you have made up a reasonable quantity. A complete section of one of the 'quality' Sundays will make enough mash to model two to three dozen ornaments. The paper should be shredded into stamp-sized pieces. First tear the sheets into quarters—several thicknesses can be done at once. Then tear these vertically into inch-wide strips, and the strips into little squares. Drop all these into a bucket or pan of cold water and leave to stand overnight. Next day stand the bucket on the cooker and bring to the boil. Simmer for an hour or so, till the pieces have disintegrated to a grey sludge. Drain in a colander, squeezing out as much water as possible. Return to bucket and add plain flour in proportions of roughly four cups to a gallon of sludge, plus a good pinch of alum, which stops the mixture going mouldy. Stir up roughly with wooden spoon. Then cook over lowest possible heat, or an asbestos mat if you have one, till the mixture is dryish, sticky and malleable—approximately one hour. As soon as it is cool enough to handle it can be used.

Model the paper mash into whatever shapes you fancy (see illustrations

Folk bird with feather tail

Papier-mâché fruits

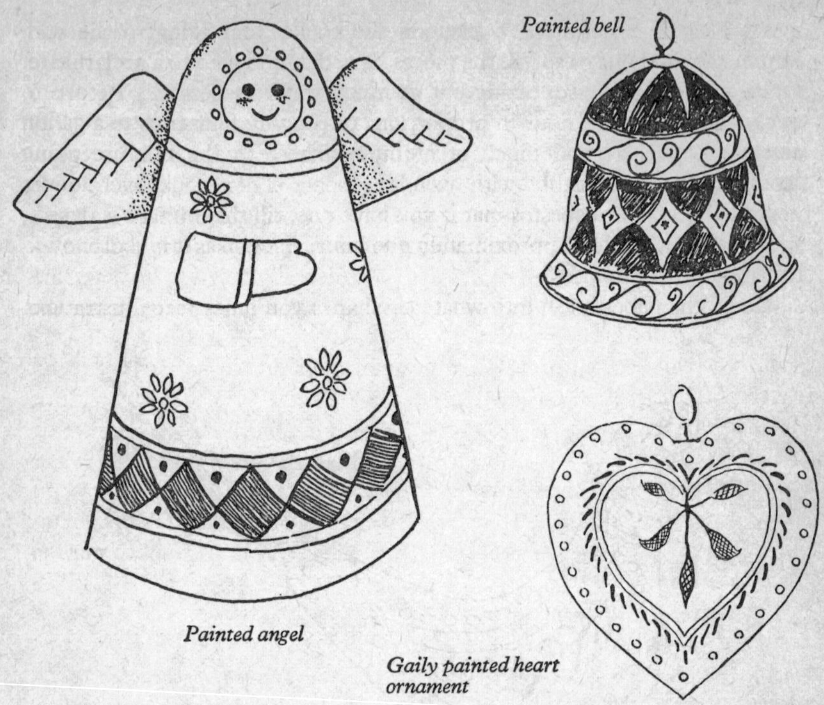

Painted bell

Painted angel

Gaily painted heart ornament

for ideas), kneading the mash well and smoothing the surfaces with damped fingers. Don't attempt elaborate modelling, or worry about a perfect finish: the pulp is being used as the core for the ornaments, and will be given a smooth surface for painting later with Polyfilla or Wallart. The shapes can be any size you like, though miniature fruit are perhaps prettier than life-size ones—papier-mâché is very light, as well as immensely strong, so quite large angels wouldn't be too heavy for the tree. Put all the pieces on baking sheets or a large piece of foil and bake in a moderate oven for one hour, or until they feel hard and dry.

This is the best time to insert wire loops for hanging them by. You can hold them by the loops for painting, and suspend them over a stick or wire to dry. Make holes for loops through small, solid shapes with a stout needle banged through with a hammer. Then thread a double thickness of wire through the hole, the loop at the top, and twist into a tiny knot at the base to hold it in place. Large flat shapes—sun faces for example—can have holes pierced through close to the edge, while stars, hearts, etc. are best supplied with a tiny brass screw eye to hang from.

Trim off any ragged edges with a sharp knife. Either Polyfilla or Wallart

(art shops) can be used to build up a smooth surface, though Wallart is harder and less porous. Mix up a stiffish mix of Polyfilla or Wallart and water in a bowl and use this to coat the little pulp shapes, working it into the cracks and hollows and using it to plump out and round off the figures nicely. I do this bit with my fingers, rolling any rounded shapes between my palms for a smooth finish. The damp plaster tends to soften the pulp somewhat, so bake the pieces again in a low oven to speed the drying out. Now sand all the shapes with medium to fine paper till nicely rounded—touch up any obvious dents or cracks with more Polyfilla or Wallart, and leave to dry. This may seem fussy but the sleeker the finish the better the pieces will look when painted and varnished. After all, they will go on for years and years so it's worth taking pains now. When you are satisfied with the finish, thread all the pieces by their loops onto a stick and suspend this between two boxes or piles of books. Now give them all a thorough coating of white undercoat. This will seal off the plaster from the paint, as well as providing the best priming coat for the paint colours. When quite dry, the ornaments are ready to paint. You can use poster colours or acrylics for this, though poster colours are cheaper. I used bright folk-art colours to paint mine—scarlet, yellow, bright blue, green, with lots of white 'feathering' and black detail. Gold spray paint makes a glamorous base for coloured decoration, and a dash of glitter. But you might prefer a different, more sophisticated palette—a quick tour round the many 'ethnic' shops which have sprung up in the big cities should give you plenty of inspiration. Paint fruit realistically—apples red shading into green or yellow patches, pears golden with brown speckling. The ornaments will probably need two coats of the base colour for good coverage—both acrylics and poster paints dry quickly. Paint yellow or green patches on apples first, then fill in with scarlet or crimson, shading the red into the first colour—if you put the green or yellow on last it will be lost in the red base colour. Any fine surface decoration should be applied with a fine brush—sable pencil for preference.

When quite dry the ornaments are ready for varnishing. This is the best part of the whole operation as the shiny varnish brings up the colours brilliantly. Almost any varnish will do, provided it's not too yellow. Polyurethane is exceptionally tough, clear picture varnish is fragile but 'water white' as the professionals say, and Humbrol clear enamel (it comes in tiny tins from toy shops, craft shops) gives a particularly luscious and sparkling finish, which looks good enough to eat. One coat is enough, but two is better still. Leave the pieces to dry completely between coats, preferably in a dust-free atmosphere. You may want to add a few details now—green leaves to the fruit, feather tails to the birds, a dash of glitter or whatever. See 'table decorations' for how to make shiny leaves from milk bottle tops, or more simply, cut leaves from green paper or felt and glue to wire stems, which are wrapped round the base of the wire loop. Feather tails can be glued to the bird's behind, or more neatly, pushed into holes bored with a stout darning needle. Small brightly coloured curling feathers (dip white feathers into water coloured with paint) look prettiest. Angels can have gauzy or shiny wings glued and pinned into place.

Note. I found my heart-shaped ornaments being snapped up to wear as pendants from a leather thong or string of wooden beads. If you want to make some to give away as pendants, use a little brass screw eye instead of a wire loop to hang them by—it looks nicer and will be stronger.

Cotton Ball Danglers

Cotton balls (like styrene balls sold at florists but much cheaper) make pleasantly textured danglers if you wrap them round tightly with string. You can paint them, or spray them gold or silver and stick them with sequins, beads, etc. But to my mind they look most attractive—like tiny Japanese paper lanterns—if you leave them string coloured, and paint on a simple holly motif.

Materials

Cotton balls in various sizes, plain string, 1 packet decorators' size (paint shops, DIY shops, ironmongers), long needle and thread, paints, brushes.

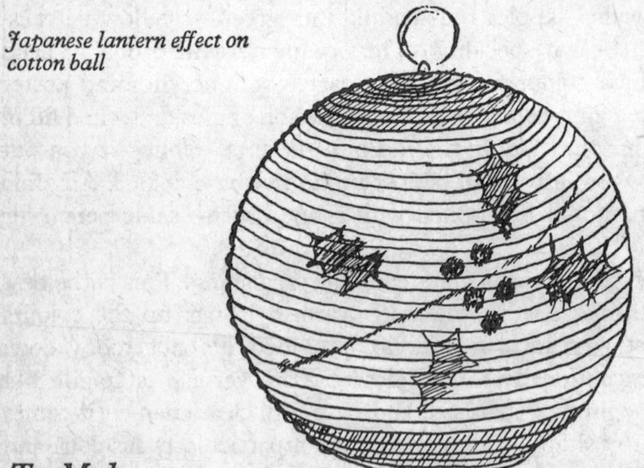

Japanese lantern effect on cotton ball

To Make

First make up a strong glue size solution. To do this, half fill a jam jar with size straight from the packet. Add enough cold water to moisten. Leave to stand a few minutes. Then pour on enough boiling water to liquefy the mixture, stirring with spoon or stick till the granules are dissolved. Use the size warm (stand it in a pan of hot water) and paint on with an old brush.

Now insert a loop to hang them by: stab a long needle right through the cotton ball and push a stout thread loop through, knotting securely at one end. Alternatively, punch a hole through and insert a wire loop. You will find it easiest to cover the ball with string in two operations, one half at a time. Cut a good long piece of string—two yards or so—fray out each end a little and coat with size by pulling it slowly under the glue-soaked brush on a pad of newspaper. Then begin winding the string from the middle of the ball towards one end—a sticky business, but not difficult—keeping the twists of string as close together as possible. If the size is thick enough you should get near-impact adhesion, with the bonus that size dries out to a splendidly stiff, lustrous finish. Press down the last little twist of string firmly and pin to hold in place while it dries. Then wrap the other half the same way. When dry—the next day—decorate in any of the ways suggested (see illustration for Japanese lantern effects). You could, of course, use coloured string instead of plain, for variety. Stick sequins, beads, etc. in place with ordinary pins or coloured hatpins.

Cotton Ball Snowmen

Using cotton balls in two sizes you can make snowmen in a couple of minutes. They look amusing as tree ornaments when given felt mufflers, hats and the usual buttons and pipe.

Cotton ball snowman

Materials

Cotton balls in medium and small sizes, long needle and thread or wire, scraps of felt, pipe cleaners, black wool, tiny buttons.

To Make

Glue a small ball onto a bigger one, or simply string them both onto a thread or wire loop, using the long needle. Leave the ends of the loop free to thread through the hat. Make the hat from painted cardboard (use one end of a cardboard tube—Smartie size) and thread the loop through the crown before glueing down securely. Cut a scrap of red or coloured felt into a muffler with fringed ends to knot round the snowman's neck. Pin buttons into place with ordinary pins. Paint the snowman's features on and stick a pipe—made from a length of pipe cleaner wrapped with black wool—into his mouth.

Note. Using the two larger sizes of cotton balls supplied, you can make identical snowmen as table decorations or to stand on the Christmas cake.

'Peppermint' Canes

I believe real peppermint canes are still sold in some of the ritzier London stores, but I haven't seen any elsewhere. The walking-stick shape and red and white stripes were such an attractive feature of Victorian Christmas trees, to judge from old prints, that I decided to copy them in Das (modelling material), paint and varnish—inedible, alas, but still pretty. Half a dozen or so of these pseudo-canes look very effective hanging from the tree, but tie them on securely because Das is brittle when dry.

'Peppermint' cane

Materials

Das modelling material (art shops, hobby shops), white undercoat, red poster paint or acrylic, masking tape, shellac or varnish, red ribbon or string.

To Make

The canes couldn't be easier to make. Roll out a long thin sausage of Das, after kneading well to make it pliable, and drive out air bubbles. Break off into twelve-inch lengths—the size of the canes should be scaled to the size of your tree—slender ones for a tiny tree, quite robust ones for a big tree. Bend the top into a crook and leave to dry hard. Paint with white undercoat and leave to dry. Cut masking tape in half—this makes it more flexible—and wrap round the cane as shown in the illustration. Paint the spaces between the tape with red paint. When dry, unpeel the masking tape and dip the whole cane—you can hold it with tweezers—into a tin of varnish or shellac. Leave to dry. Tie a red ribbon or bit of red string to each one.

Punched and Painted Tin

Common-or-garden tins can be re-cycled into shiny tree decorations. Cut the tin into decorative shapes (peacocks, butterflies, angels, fish, etc.), punch patterns into them, and paint with oil colours in varnish for a gaudy glitter reminiscent of Mexican folk tinware. The only special equipment needed is a pair of shears tough enough to cut tin. Don't use kitchen scissors—it will ruin them. I tried a widely advertised brand of all purpose cutters (Snips, from ironmongers, Woolworth's) and found them very efficient.

Warning. Cut tin is sharp, so proceed with care, and don't let small children help. Rubbing the sharp edges on carborundum paper will blunt them somewhat but even so keep them out of small children's way. (Ironmongers and Woolworth's stock carborundum paper.)

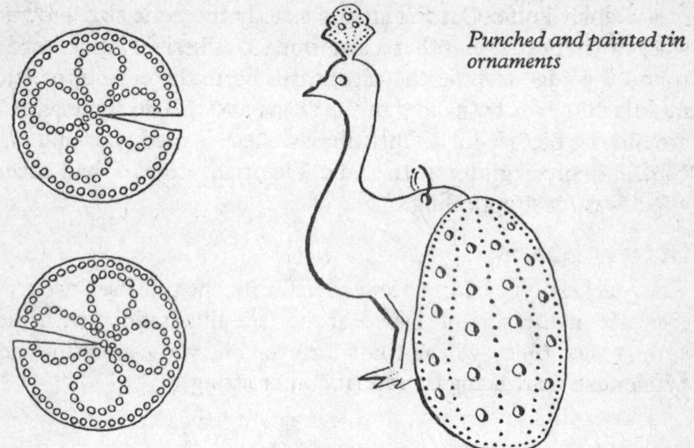

Punched and painted tin ornaments

Materials

Tins, Snips cutters, blunt and sharp nails for punching, hammer, plank to hammer on, clear varnish, oil colours (Alizarin crimson and sap green are particularly good colours for this).

Method

Prepare tins first: remove labels and cut into flat sheets. Draw shapes on these with a felt pen, then cut round with the shears—it's best to cut rough shapes first, then tackle the finer work later. For a 3-D effect, simple shapes like bells, circles, etc., can be slotted into each other, as shown in the illustration. Use blunt and sharp nails to punch embossed patterns or holes in the tin shapes. These add surface interest and catch the light prettily. Punch from one side and perforate from the other to even out the cockling of the metal. You can also cut slashed patterns with a sharp penknife, tapping it hard with the hammer.

Wipe the surfaces with a rag and turps to remove grease and fingermarks before painting. Dissolve the paint colours in a little varnish and apply with a small soft brush. Using paint in varnish means you keep the brilliance of the tin through the transparent colour. Alternatively, you could paint with bright opaque enamels. Leave to dry thoroughly. Thread with wire loops.

'Picture' Ornaments

Any Christmassy cut-outs—Santa figures, angels, etc. from old Christmas cards—or even brightly coloured stickers, can be converted into tree ornaments by pasting them to a cardboard circle or oval covered on both sides in bright felt. Use a glass to trace off circles and cut round with Snips or a Stanley knife. Cut felt shapes exactly the same size and stick on both sides with Bostik or other clear impact adhesive. Stick cord or ribbon round the edge to hide the cardboard. Paste the cut-out or sticker in the middle of one or both sides of the shape and dab on some paste and glitter around the picture for a Christmassy effect. I used shocking pink felt, red cord and silver glitter with some Victorian scraps I had saved, and the effect was most appealing.

Straw Stars

The quickest type of straw star to make for the tree uses two triangles held together in the star of David shape (see illustration) with blobs of red sealing wax. They will not last for ever but you can easily make another batch next year. Hang by red ribbon or string.

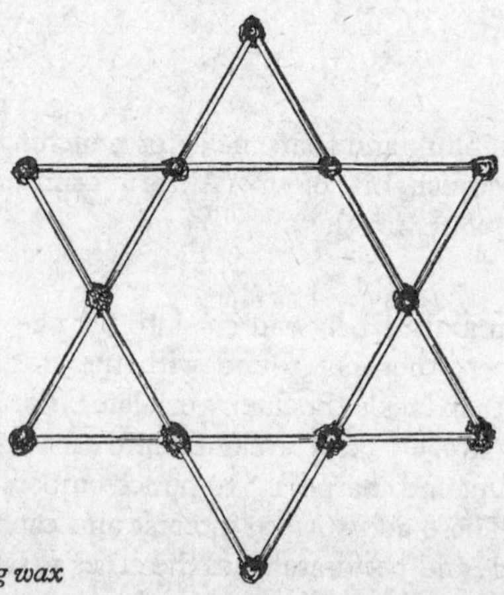

Straw star with sealing wax

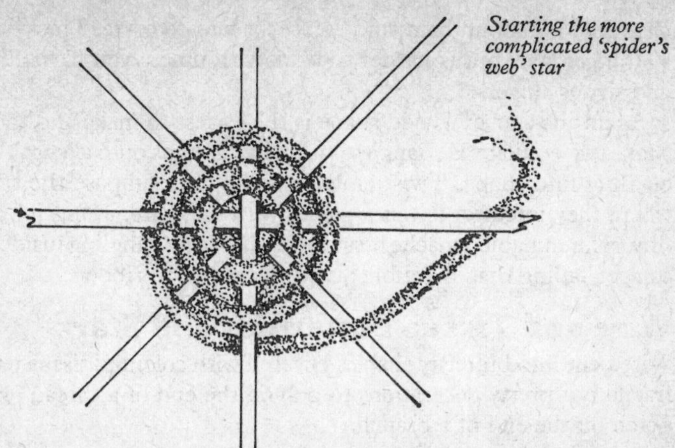

Starting the more complicated 'spider's web' star

Fancier straw stars are made by laying four straws of equal length on top of each other, and winding cotton round rather as a spider spins its web, winding the thread under one straw, over the next and so on, occasionally varying the arrangement so that the thread goes under the ones it previously went over, and vice versa. Do this till the star feels firm—three or four rows will be enough. Now make a similar star in the same way, using shorter straws of equal length, and finally join the two stars together with more thread wound round as before. Trim off the ends of the straws to sharp points. A red ribbon rosette centred with a small fir cone looks pretty wired to the middle of the star. Hang the star by a long thread loop. *Note.* Use coloured plastic drinking straws (but not with sealing wax) for stars with a quite different look. Trim the ends to points.

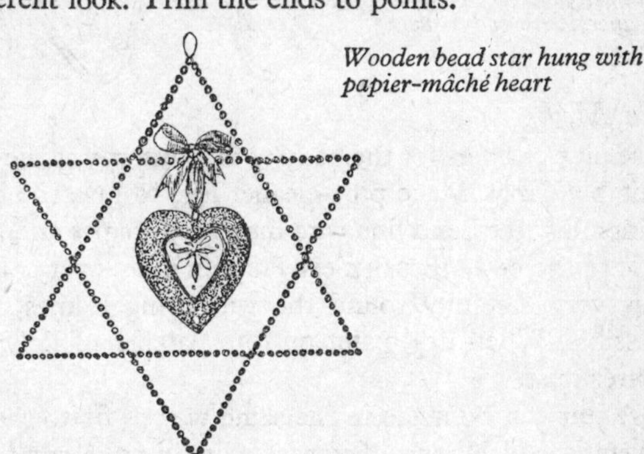

Wooden bead star hung with papier-mâché heart

Wooden Bead Stars

Coloured wooden beads threaded on wire and bent into star shapes have a cheerful look about them, and don't take long to make. Thicker wire makes a stronger star, but is harder to work with unless you have cutters, pliers and strong fingers.

Again the star of David shape is the easiest to make and the strongest. Make two equilateral triangles by threading beads onto a length of wire and bending into shape. Twist ends securely. Superimpose the triangles and where they intersect fasten together with fine wire. Hang by a ribbon. A tiny painted papier-mâché heart looks charming dangling inside the beaded star, or failing that, a bauble or two threaded on ribbon.

Wire and Tissue Butterflies and Stars

Wire bent into butterfly shapes, covered with coloured tissue paper, makes fragile but pretty decorations to bob on the end of a thread or better still perch on the end of a branch.

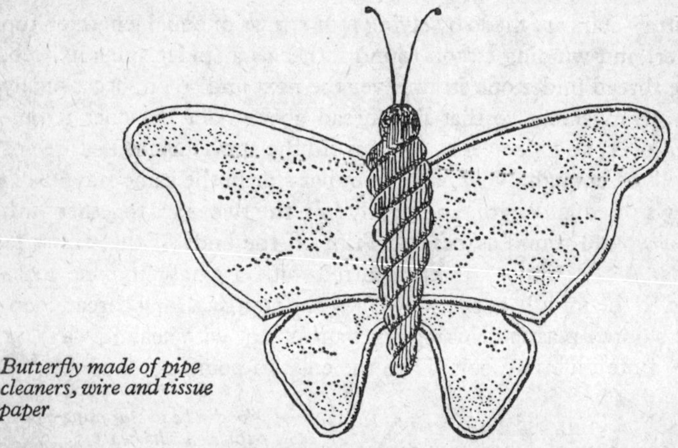

Butterfly made of pipe cleaners, wire and tissue paper

To Make

Use pipe cleaners for the body of the butterfly as they are stronger and look suitably furry. Make pipe-cleaner legs to give the butterfly something to cling on with. Bend fine wire into wing shapes and attach these to either side of the body. Brush clear Polycell paste over coloured tissue and wrap this very carefully round the wire wing frames, keeping it as taut as possible. When dry, paint on thin patches of Polycell and sprinkle with glitter dust.

A star can be made in the same way to fix to the top of the tree. The advantage of this sort of star is its lightness. Again the star of David shape is the most suitable. Cover with white tissue, and sprinkle liberally with silver glitter dust.

String and Hessian Angels

I borrowed this idea from some decorations I saw in a German shop. The homespun effect of these soberly coloured little figures contrasted very effectively with the usual Christmas glitter. Use scraps of hessian, or plain sacking, and ordinary string to make them.

String and hessian angel

To Make

Cut out the basic shape in cardboard. Glue hessian or sackcloth with glue size over the whole shape, back and front. Use two shades of hessian—brown and blue, or maroon—or paint the sackcloth when the size has dried. Press under heavy books to flatten. Using plain string brushed over with size, make the curly flourishes shown in the illustration. Stick on a tiny pink circle for a face, with features drawn in Indian ink. Punch a hole at the top and thread a wire loop through.

Holders for Sweets, Small Presents

Felt Boots

Make these from scraps of felt (you can buy offcuts cheaply by the pound, see Suppliers' Index). Cut boot shapes in red felt, or brightly contrasting colours—pink one side, yellow the other. Stitch together by machine. Decorate with cottonwool, Santa stickers, ribbon bows, etc. Hang from thread or wire loops if the contents are light enough, otherwise lay them across the branches.

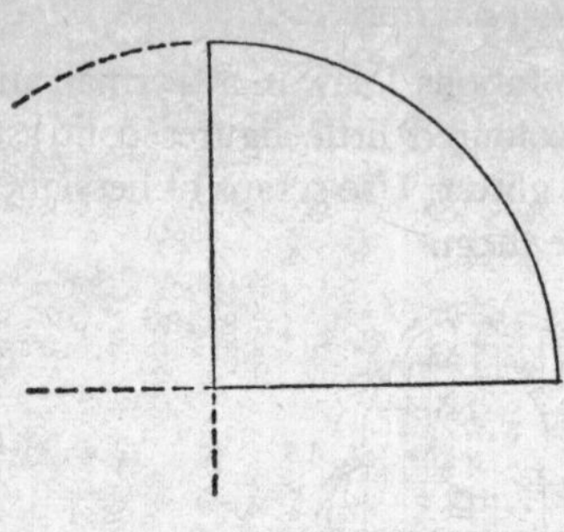

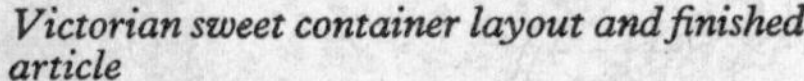

Victorian sweet container layout and finished article

Cardboard Cones

A Victorian idea, and pretty as a container for sweets. Cut cone shapes from thin white cardboard and staple or glue into shape. Bind shiny sellotape round and round as shown. Stick a frill of paper doily round the top, make a wire handle to hang it by and fill with sweets.

Quickies

Gilded Walnuts

Spray walnuts gold. When dry, cut a wire loop, insert both ends into the hole at one end of the nut, twist round, then bring the loop round the nut and twist again to make a small loop to hang it by. Gilded nuts are traditional, and always look charming.

Silver Springs

You can cut circles of cooking foil into corkscrew shapes to bob up and down on the tree. These are quite effective if you don't overdo it. Cut small circles—coffee-cup size and then cut round and round continuously as if peeling an apple. Open out gently and pinch the thicker end over the tree to hold in place.

Brass Curtain Rings

If you have any large brass curtain rings, or gilt bangles, use these to frame a shiny bauble, or even a sparkling brooch or earring. Hang the centrepiece from a thread or wire loop, and finish off with a red ribbon bow.

Miniature Paper Chains

One Christmas Eve, faced with a decidedly underprivileged-looking tree, I sat down and made yards of tiny paper chains, coloured links interspersed with silver ones (cooking foil stuck with PVA—I used Evostik wood adhesive), to swag from branch to branch. I used the standard paper strips sold for chain making, but cut each strip into four, which meant a lot more sticking but suited the scale of the tree better. Foil must be stuck with PVA.

Plastic Doilies

Should you have any small lacy plastic mats, spray them gold both sides and hang by a ribbon. Useful for filling up gaps between branches.

Making the Most of Your (lop-sided, ragged, stunted or yellowing) Tree

So few Christmas trees on sale these days come anywhere near the ideal springy green pyramid-shape that one hears of people being driven to astonishing shifts—like the man I heard on the radio telling us how to thatch a chicken wire cone with tufts of pine-needles from the cupressus tree. If you are the sort of person who tends to leave tree buying till the last minute, it is as well to be ready with decorations which disguise imperfections as well as laying on colour and sparkle.

Lop-sided

Stand the tree in a corner, turn the best side to face the room and chop off any branches or branch tips which jut wildly out of place. Trim the topmost tip if it is too long. Fix a star to the top and stick foil springs on the ends of the cut-off branches.

Thin and Ragged

One of the commonest flaws of Christmas trees is simply too few branches, which leaves yawning spaces between that are always difficult to fill. Use lots of swagging—red furry ropes, tinsel ropes, miniature paper chains—to fill the gaps between the branches and hang quite large but airy looking decorations—stars, gilt doilies, tissue butterflies, etc.—in the spaces. Lengthen the threads too so they hang midway, not close to the branch.

Yellowing

The best disguise for a yellowing tree, or indeed any slightly sorry-looking tree, is lots of frosting. My maternal grandmother, a champion make-do-and-mender, once showed me how to do this with whitewash and soap flakes. The up-to-date equivalent I suppose would be white emulsion and soap powder and/or flakes mixed with silver glitter. To frost—simply slosh paint artistically (lay paper on the floor first) over all the tops of the branches to simulate snow, and then sprinkle generously with the frosting while still wet. You will then have a delicately ghostly tree against which all your coloured decorations look very fine.

Decorations for the House, Table, Children's Parties, etc.

Do people ever find time to undertake the Christmas transformations featured in women's magazines—whole walls hung with foil and coloured paper, ceilings dripping with baubles and streamers? Perhaps I am a defeatist, but my own guess is that most householders settle thankfully for something less ambitious in the way of general decorations. A wreath for the front door, plenty of holly, one or two eyecatching special decorations, and an extra effort for the Christmas table setting. In this section I shall be featuring some not-too-elaborate ideas on these lines. The one occasion, it seems to me, that warrants a big extra effort is a children's party—children love something spectacular and unexpected—so I have included some ideas to help make the party go.

Holly Wreath

Holly wreaths to hang on the front door are so easy to make it seems absurd to pay several pounds for a bought one, especially if you live in the country where holly can still be had for the picking. (Use clippers, and don't savage the bush.) All you need, apart from a good quantity of holly, is a wire frame made from two circles of heavy gauge wire (you could use wire coat hangers) joined together by more wire, as in the accompanying diagram. Use pliers to bend the wire—men are better at this, as they have stronger hands. Thread sprigs of holly in and out of the wire to build up a nice bushy shape—holly is so prickly it sticks to itself, so you shouldn't need extra aids like crumpled chicken wire folded over the frame. Add glossy dark laurel, ivy or evergreen to the wreath for contrast and variety. Fir cones dipped in white paint, then sprayed with gold, look pretty wired to the wreath here and there, using fine wire. Or wrap shiny red ribbon round it, finishing off with a big bow at the top. You can hang a cluster of shiny baubles inside the wreath, or a frosted gold star, but I think they are decorative enough just as they are.

Quickie Wreath

An ultra-quick way to make a front door wreath which doesn't call for pliers, wire or manual strength, is to set sprigs of greenery—holly, laurel, ivy, spruce, even privet—anything will do so long as it is green and shiny—into a ring of plaster of Paris. The only snag with plaster wreaths is their weight, so don't make it too big—15 inches across is about right—unless you have a good strong knocker or other door fixing to attach it to.

Wire frame for holly wreath made from coathanger wire

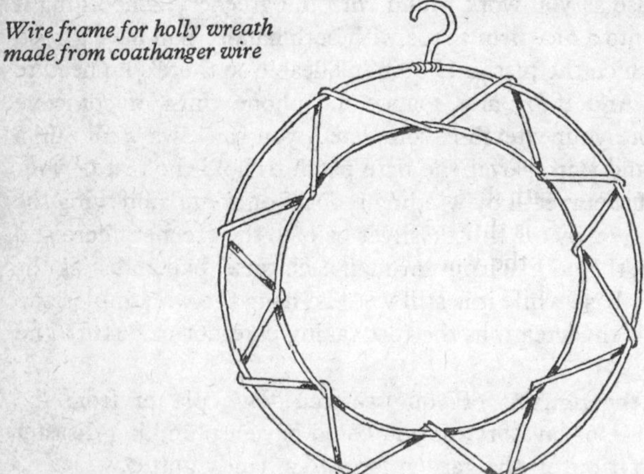

Materials

5 lb. bag of plaster of Paris (Boots), short sprigs of greenery (approximately a bucketful, but pick too much rather than too little) with a bit of stalk on them, sheet of plastic (open up a large plastic bag), two large mixing bowls or buckets.

To Make

Plaster of Paris doesn't set solid in an instant, as inexperienced users are apt to imagine. All the same you should have everything set out and ready to hand before embarking on your wreath. Spread a sheet of plastic out on the table, make a pile of greenery on the right, drape an old towel (to wipe your hands on) over a chair back and you are ready to begin. The base for a 15-inch wreath will require approximately 1 quart of water and most of your bag of plaster. Measure the quart of water into one of your bowls or buckets. Fill the other bowl or bucket with clean water and have it standing by to rinse out your mixing bowl or bucket with. Now begin pouring the plaster of Paris in a steady stream into the measured quart, stirring with your free hand or a stick to break up lumps. Stop when it reaches the consistency of thick cream. Pour the plaster carefully on to your plastic sheet to make a big, roughly circular dollop. Immediately tip clean water into your mixing bowl or bucket to stop the plaster hardening over it. Now return to your dollop of wet plaster. Begin shaping it with both hands into a ring the size you want your wreath to be. At first the plaster will slop about and refuse to be coaxed into shape, but suddenly you will notice it firming up and at this point you need to work coolly but quickly. Begin sticking springs of greenery, stalk downwards, into the plaster, arranging them so they bush out prettily and hide the white plaster base. Keep shaping the ring base as you work round with the greenery, smoothing it and building it up into a nice firm shape with both hands. You have a good 5 minutes during which the plaster is quite malleable so there's no need to get into a fluster. And if by any chance the phone rings or someone interrupts you before your wreath is completed, you can always mix up a little more plaster and slap it over the bare patch to hold the rest of your greenery. Finish off the wreath by winding red ribbon round and tying the ends in a grand bow, or by tying little silver balls to the greenery here and there. Alternatively, thread a hairpin through each tinsel ball and stick the ends into the plaster base while it is still wet. To hang the wreath up, loop twine or wire round the wreath at the top, taking care not to disturb the greenery too much.

Note. Don't pour the remains of your watered-down plaster from the mixing bowl into sink or lavatory, or you could have a plumbing disaster on your hands. Tip it out in the garden, or into a handy gutter.

Kissing Ball

This is one of the prettiest traditional decorations—a ball of holly and mistletoe hung strategically in an archway or from a ceiling light to make the most of the special mistletoe dispensation. Hence the name. A kissing ball should be as pretty as ribbons, baubles, etc. can make it.

Materials

Large ball of plasticine, hair net or cotton net saved from a bag of oranges, hairpins, holly and mistletoe, baubles, 1 yard of wide red ribbon.

To Make

Make this as near Christmas as you can so the holly is still fresh and gleaming. Stick the ball of plasticine in the hair net or cotton net bag. Push sprigs of holly of roughly the same length into the plasticine all over to make a firm rounded shape about a foot in diameter. Shiny baubles can be pushed in here and there, using hair pins threaded through the wire loops. The vital sprig of mistletoe goes into the bottom of the ball, where it can be seen easily. Wrap wire round the top of the net securely to make an invisible loop, then thread the red ribbon through this, and tie a handsome bow. If

Kissing ball

you don't like the idea of knocking a nail into your paintwork to hang the ball upon, use one of those stick-on plastic door hooks.

Christmassy Floral Effects

A sparkling Christmassy arrangement of leaves and flowers in gold, white and silver, looks handsome flanked by candles on the hall table or sideboard, and a smaller version makes a graceful Christmas present. They don't take long to do, and give you a chance to make use of all sorts of oddments lying about the house—dusty, dried or plastic flowers, sprays of leaves gathered on country walks.

Sprayed and painted flowers, leaves and grasses

Materials

Dried leaves, flowers, grasses, plastic flowers, container, plasticine or chicken wire or styrene ball, white gloss paint, gold and/or silver spray paint.

To Make

The container can be a regular vase, or a small basket, even a plastic flower pot sprayed gold and tied with ribbon. Wedge the plasticine, styrene ball or chicken wire into the bottom of the container to hold all your stems securely. Spray beech leaves, and any dried flower or seed heads which have that withered, dusty look, gold or silver. Paint plastic flowers with white gloss to look like white china—leave to dry before use. Sprays of silvery honesty are perfect for this sort of arrangement, likewise any golden wheat ears you might have salvaged from a harvest festival—these probably need fine wire threaded up the stems. Arrange the leaves, flowers, etc. by pushing the stems into the plasticine or whatever you are using to build up a fine, dramatic clump—this isn't the type of decoration that calls for studied Japanese subtleties.

Six-pointed Cardboard Star

This is one of the most effective shapes to make from cardboard. Covered in silver foil (or cooking foil) it looks very fine hanging just inside the front door. It is really solid geometry in terms of cardboard, and schoolchildren are understandably deft at assembling shapes like these. My twelve-year-old daughter, Daisy, made mine in a couple of hours, and a neat and accurate piece of work it is too.

Materials

Light cardboard (shirt boards are excellent), Stanley knife or sharp scissors, geometry tools, PVA adhesive, gummed brown paper strip, silver foil.

To Make

Measure out and draw the component shapes of the star on the cardboard—6 pyramid shapes and a cube—as shown in the diagram. Our star was a large one—14 inches from apex to apex—but yours can be made smaller by scaling down all the measurements by the same amount. Cut out the shapes with the knife or scissors. Lightly score all fold lines by running the knife point along a ruler. Bend at fold lines. Assemble the six pyramid shapes and cube by pasting gummed strip over the joins. You can paste it along the joins for strength, or simply stick short lengths across to hold them together. The foil covering will hide all this. Cut silver foil shapes to cover the pyramids—using one card shape as a pattern and allowing ¼ inch extra all round for overlaps. Brush PVA (you must use PVA-type adhesives for sticking metal foil) thinly over the cardboard shapes and paste down the cover sections, working them flat and smooth with a table knife—as for icing. Trim away any surplus overlaps neatly with a razor blade. To

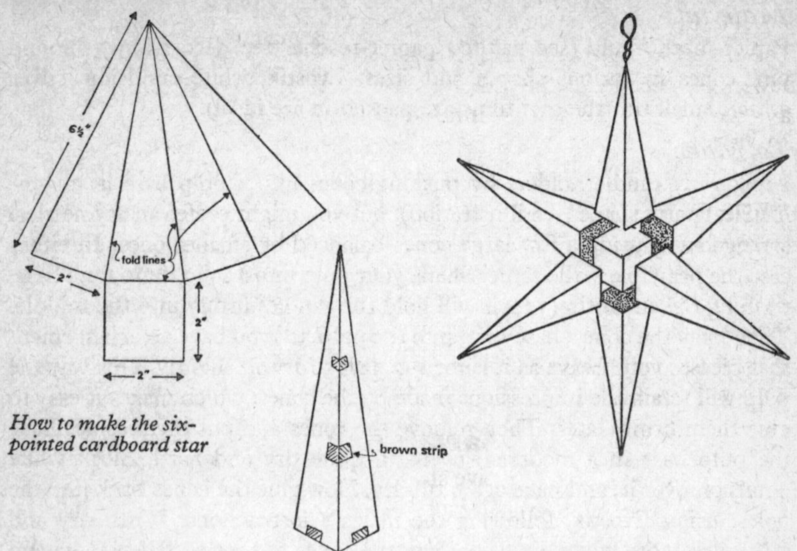

How to make the six-pointed cardboard star

assemble the star, coat the base of each pyramid (which won't have been covered with foil) and each face of the cube thinly with PVA and leave till the adhesive becomes clear. Then press together firmly, till stuck fast. Pierce the apex of one pyramid with a needle and thread a wire loop through for hanging the star by. You can hang a string of baubles from each point (if you have enough baubles to spare) or wind ribbons or red furry ropes or greenery round the star as further decoration.

Fir Cone Candle Holders

If you live anywhere near a forestry reserve, or coniferous wood, you will

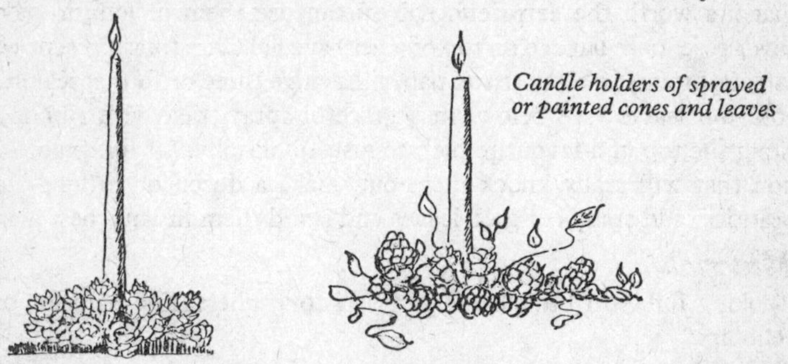
Candle holders of sprayed or painted cones and leaves

find fir and pine cones lying about in drifts. They make pretty holders for red candles to stand on the mantelpiece or table.

Materials

Papier-mâché pulp (see painted papier-mâché tree decorations), fir and pine cones in various shapes and sizes, Evostik, white emulsion, silver glitter, small tin (the sort films are packed in are ideal).

To Make

I made my candle holders by pushing cones into a pulp base in a symmetrical daisy shape (see illustration), but you might prefer an asymetrical arrangement, using a few large cones balanced by smaller ones. In either case the principle is the same. Shape your pulp into a solid lump for a base, pushing the small tin (which will hold the candle) firmly into the middle. Then push the cones, base first, into the pulp, till you have an arrangement that pleases you. Leave as it is for 1–2 days to dry off slightly. This way the pulp will retain the impressions made by the cones, which makes it easy to glue them firmly later. Then remove the cones and put them aside. Bake the pulp base in a moderate oven till quite dry and hard. Slosh white emulsion over it, and bake again till dry. Now glue the cones back into the holes, using Evostik, following the maker's instructions. When dry and solid, dab more white emulsion over the cones to suggest fallen snow and sprinkle with glitter while wet. Glue candle holder into place. Decorate further with sprigs of holly, formed into a wreath round the base, or tiny baubles threaded on fine wire and woven in and out of the cones. Another idea which looks particularly attractive, and costs nothing, is sprays of silver and gold foil leaves (made from milk bottle tops) woven in and out of the cones. They catch the light from the candles very prettily.

Cooking Foil Roses

It takes a little perseverance to get these just right, but the materials are so cheap and the results so exceptionally pretty—just like roses, only silver—that it's worth the extra effort. You can use them in lots of ways—one silver rose looks superb on top of a very special Christmas present wrapped in dark brown or black tissue paper. Arrange three or four roses plus some gold foil leaves (see below) in a graceful spray, tied with ribbon, to lay along the top of a favourite picture instead of holly. Or for a table decoration that will really knock them out, make a dozen or so long-stemmed beauties, add sprays of gold leaves and stand them in your best glass vase.

Materials

Cooking foil, stiff but pliable wire, scissors, pliers, fine wire for binding, sellotape.

To Make

Cut petal shapes from foil. Don't give yourself a headache trying to make each one exactly like the rest, because the shape of the rose comes more from artful pinching and manipulation of the foil than from precision cutting. Each rose takes about nine petals—add more for a full-blown effect—and you can cut the centre petals about ¼ inch shorter than the outer ones. An average petal measures approximately 2 inches across by approximately 1¾ down. Now with pliers cut a length of wire 6–9 inches long—depending on what you want to do with the rose—and bend one end over to make a small loop. This loop is what you build up the rose around, and prevents the petals slipping off the end. Take the first petal and curl it tightly round on itself over the loop, squeezing the base firmly into place round the wire stalk. Curl the second petal round the first, but more loosely. The third petal is centred on the gap between the two sides of the second petal. And so on, till your rose has blossomed out to a respectable size. The shapeliness of your foil rose will depend very much on your sense of what a real rose looks like and how accurately your fingers can curl and coax the foil into reproducing this. If you have the knack, you're away, if you haven't, well, see what a little practice can do. To finish off your rose and secure it on its stalk, wrap a couple of twists of fine wire round the base of the flower and then bind with sellotape. Further the illusion, if you like, by wrapping the wire stalk with a long narrow strip (bias binding width) of crêpe or tissue paper in green, white, or—most dramatic—black.

Silver and Gold Foil Leaves

Collect a box full of milk bottle tops, washing and rinsing carefully in warm water and detergent to remove milk fat. The tops should be removed in one piece, don't keep them if they are ripped. Cut off the crimped edge round the tops with small scissors and smooth the disc flat with a fingernail. Cut into leaf shapes. Cut short lengths of fine wire and strips of

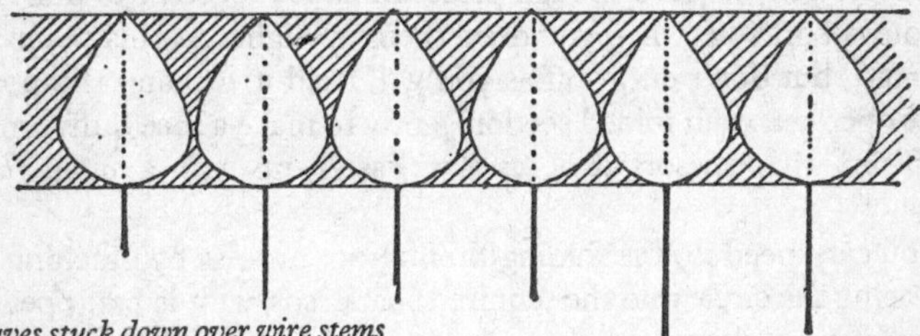

Foil leaves stuck down over wire stems with brown paper backings

brown paper about 1¼ inches wide and 12 inches long. Coat the paper and one side of the foil leaves with PVA. Lay the wire stems along the paper as shown in the illustration. When the PVA becomes clear, press leaves on top of the wires all the way down the strip of paper and weight under books. When quite dry, cut round the foil shapes to make a foil leaf with a brown paper backing and wire stem running up the middle. Crease veins into the leaf with your fingernail, and bend it slightly to give it a naturalistic curve. The stems can be twisted together to make one continuous wire of leaves branching out left and right (this makes a pretty small wreath to hang on the tree or even adorn a little girl's head). Or join together two or three at a time to make a spray. The foil can be painted with oil colours dissolved in varnish to achieve metallic coloured effects.

Tissue Paper Pompoms

These can be made quickly and easily—get the children to help—from coloured tissue paper. They look prettiest in plain white or white mixed with a pale pastel shade, and a fetching way to use them is suspended from the ceiling (use sellotape which won't mark) in a sort of canopy above the tree.

Materials

Several packets of coloured or white tissue paper, scissors, needle and thread.

To Make

Fold one or two sheets of tissue several times—as if you were folding a newspaper—to give you a narrow strip several layers thick. Pencil circle shapes along your length of folded tissue, using cups, lids or anything handy to draw round (the pompoms can be any size from golf ball to grapefruit) and cut round the outline, cutting through all the layers simultaneously. Go on till you have accumulated a fair pile of tissue circles. Now begin folding these (children are handy at this) in half, then in half again to give you the correct shape. To make pompoms, thread a long bit of strong cotton on a needle and stitch through the points of your folded circles till you have enough pieces threaded together to fluff up into a nice round pompom when you draw them up tight. At this point secure your thread, but don't cut it off as you will need it to hang the pompom by. Now open out each folded section gently to make a nice fluffy, rounded shape. Trim with scissors if necessary. Fasten up with a small piece of sellotape.

Note. You can speed up the folding/fluffing-out process by pinching rather than creasing the circle into the required shape, so that it is half opened out already. Young children are not quite so handy at this, however, so what you gain on the swings you may lose on the roundabout.

Christmas Crackers

Home-made crackers are a real money saver, especially if there is a children's party coming up. They don't look quite so streamlined as the bought variety, but you can compensate by including imaginative mottoes and attractive little toys or gifts chosen to suit the particular child—or adult.

Materials

Sheets of crêpe paper in various colours, plain white paper for linings, cardboard rolls (toilet and kitchen paper rolls), a selection of tiny gifts and mottoes (see below for suggestions), 'snappers', glue, string.

To Make

Cut all the cardboard rolls to the same size with a sharp knife. Perforate round middle of tube with needle to make it pull apart better. Insert little gifts, which can be wrapped for extra excitement. Cut crêpe paper cover and linings as shown in the illustration. If you have time, pink the ends of the crêpe covers with pinking shears. Arrange the cracker components as shown, roll up smoothly and stick the paper cover to the lining with a spot of glue. Gather up the crêpe paper either side of the cardboard roll, crimping it as neatly as possible and tie securely with string or button thread. Decorate the crackers with coloured motifs cut from old Christmas cards—angels, Santas, Christmas trees, etc.—and stuck on with a dab of glue. Add a sprinkle of glitter.

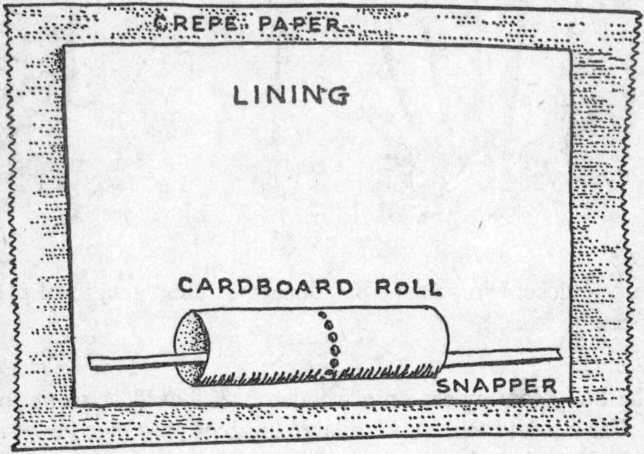

Making the Christmas cracker

Cracker Gift Ideas

For children: transfer sets, plastic animals, tiny rings, bead bracelets, hair slides, miniature cars. For the ladies: miniature lipsticks, eyeshadows, tiny scent bottles, bath bubbles and cubes, Woolworth's jewellery. For the gents: cigarillos, cuff links, dice, rolls of film.

Hessian Tablecloth

One quickly made idea guaranteed to raise everyone's spirits is a brilliant red tablecloth. It is an exciting background for silver, glass, china, etc. Make it from hessian, which comes in 6-foot widths, and is still one of the cheapest materials available (see Suppliers' Index). One width will cover most tables generously—all you need to do is machine up hems at both ends. Centre it with one of the pieces below, and plain white candles in your best candleholders, and you will have a really memorable setting for your Christmas lunch or dinner for very little trouble or expense.

Note. The hessian cloth can be washed afterwards, but be prepared for some shrinking. Provide paper napkins.

Holly Centrepieces

Nothing gives such an instant feeling of Christmas as lots of holly, so why not make the most of it? A centrepiece—round or elongated to suit the shape of your table—of shiny green holly stuck with slender white tapers takes only a few minutes to make.

Holly decorations for the Christmas table

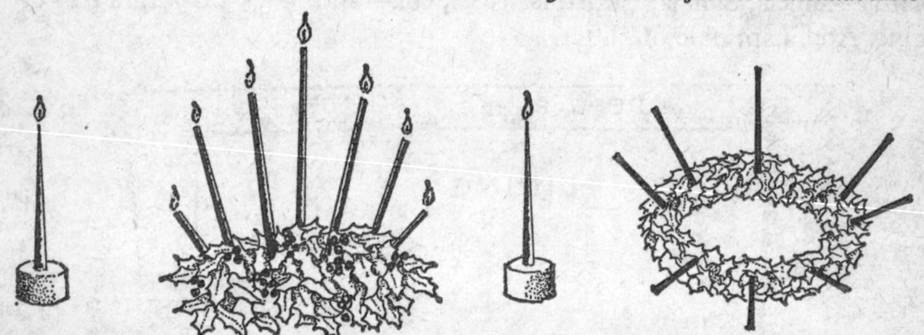

Materials

Plasticine or chickenwire, round breadboard or short length of planking, holly, tapers.

To Make

Mount the holly centrepiece on a wooden breadboard or plank for convenience. For a round table, stick a large lump of plasticine in the middle of a smallish breadboard, and spike all over with holly in a rounded shape till the plasticine is quite hidden. Drive narrow holes in here and there with a knitting needle and embed tapers firmly in these. For a long narrow centrepiece on an oblong table, begin with a long sausage of plasticine and cover with crumpled chickenwire. Stick with holly, adding ivy, tufts of evergreen and laurel, if your holly supplies aren't adequate. Embed white tapers as before.

Poinsettia

Plants do make lovely table decorations and a nicely shaped, medium height poinsettia in full bloom can be dressed up in a minute by spraying the pot with gold paint. Salvage a pretty piece of ribbon and tie this round the pot, finishing with a generous bow.

Candle in a Basket

A plain red candle, not mottled or sculpted, sturdy enough to stand on its own makes an attractive, casual-looking centrepiece if you stand it in a shallow basketwork platter, surrounded by Christmas greenery and gilded walnuts.

Tiered Tree Centrepiece

Anyone with a jig saw in their tool cupboard could knock up this attractive little tiered tree centrepiece, to decorate with little Christmas figures, small presents, sweets, nuts, crackers, etc. In Germany, where brightly painted, much more elaborate versions of the tree were traditional Christmas centrepieces, they used to set them with candles and brightly painted little wooden figures, houses and animals. Raid the toy cupboard!

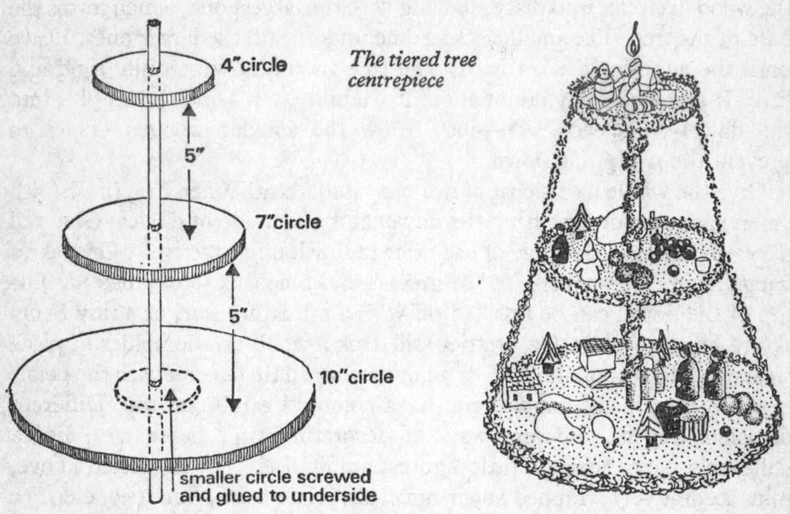

The tiered tree centrepiece

Materials

Enough offcuts of ⅜- or ½-inch chipboard or plywood to cut three circles, of 4-inch, 7-inch and 10-inch diameters. One-foot length of ½-inch wooden dowel (available from any do-it-yourself shop), ½-inch screws, bradawl, drill and ½-inch wood bit, Thixofix adhesive, undercoat, green enamel, red paper rope to decorate the tree.

To Make

The tree is made on the same principle as a wedding-cake stand—in fact, anyone who has a wedding-cake stand could use that instead. With a compass draw three circles, of 4-inch, 7-inch and 10-inch diameters on the offcut ply or chipboard. Cut round with the jig saw. Neaten edges with sandpaper. From remaining scraps of wood cut three small circles (or squares if cutting small circles is too difficult) 2 inches in diameter. With the drill and woodworking bit, drill ½-inch holes through the middle of all the circles, including the three small ones, which are needed to keep the tree from wobbling on its centre pole. Make four small holes with a bradawl in the 2-inch circles for screw sites. Glue small circles to the larger ones with Thixofix, following the maker's instructions and matching the drilled holes exactly. When the Thixofix is dry and the circles are stuck, screw them to the larger circles, using the bradawl holes as a guide (see diagram). Now mark off points on the length of dowel where the circles are to be glued in place (see diagram). Coat these with Thixofix and tape the wooden circles into place, starting with the largest one, which forms the base of the tree. The small circles come underneath the larger ones. Leave until the adhesive has set hard. The tree should now be quite rigid and firm. If you are in any doubt about its stability, tap ½-inch panel pins into the dowel—one each side—just below the smaller wooden circles to prevent them slipping down.

Give the whole tree a coat of ordinary undercoat. When dry, finish with green enamel, not forgetting the dowel and underside of circles. Glue red paper rope round the edge of each tier to finish off attractively. Or make a fringe from crêpe paper—red or green—and glue this round instead. The top of the dowel can be finished off with a miniature star, or a tiny Santa figure glued in place. Or, prettier still, tack a small candle holder in place (make this from a pill box lid, or a flower-shaped tin cut-out with the petals bent up to grip the candle) and fix a coloured candle on top. Different occasions suggest different ways of decorating your tiered tree. For a children's party, arrange little figures, animals, etc., as suggested above, plus decoratively wrapped sugar mice, chocolate coins, Smarties, etc. For an adult occasion set a few nightlights burning here and there (taking care that they don't burn the tier immediately above) and arrange liqueur chocolates, small cigars, chocolate mints, etc., in tempting rows.

Children's Party Trimmings

Balloon Clown

As a change from the mandatory bunch of balloons—gorgeous as they are—why not make a balloon clown figure to stand in one corner, or even in the middle of the table? Don't spend too much time making it beautifully because it will soon be torn to pieces, and anyway small children don't register such niceties.

Materials

Five sausage-shaped balloons, one round balloon, clown's hat, packets of white or yellow crêpe paper, packet of red paper for the ruff, poster paints, a pair of shoes or slippers.

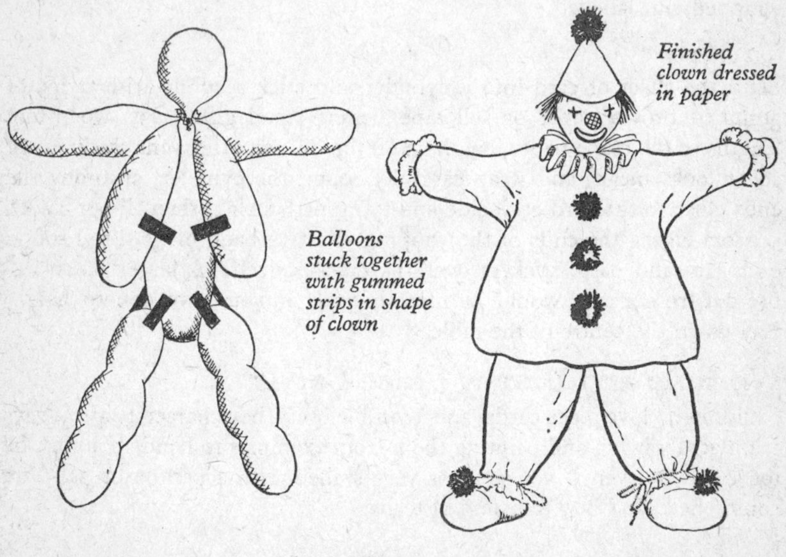

Balloons stuck together with gummed strips in shape of clown

Finished clown dressed in paper

To Make

Inflate the balloons and tie together as in the diagram. You can tie a few more sausage ones round the middle if you favour a paunchy clown. These will need to be sellotaped down to keep them in place. Gather up lengths of crêpe paper to make billowing sleeves and pant legs and tie these in place top and bottom with string. Make a loose smock top with more crêpe paper and fasten this round the clown's neck. Pin the sides to keep them anchored down but take care not to puncture the balloons. Make a generous ruff by gathering a long strip of red crêpe paper down the middle and tying round the clown's neck. Glue the clown's hat on top of his balloon head. Paint in clownish features—red nose, black star eyes, ridiculous arched brows, and a giant rubber-band mouth—with poster paints. Anchor the feet in large slippers. Tether if necessary, using string and tin tacks.

Giant Cracker

This looks promising laid down the middle of the party tea table, and is a good way of concealing the small presents till you are ready to hand them round. You can make it very rapidly. No bangs, of course.

Materials

Sheet of flexible cardboard approximately 2 foot by 2 foot, packet of red crêpe paper, string, coloured ribbon, Christmas stickers, gold foil, Bostik, sellotape or gummed brown paper strip, selection of small presents, wrapped and labelled.

To Make

Bend the sheet of card into a cylinder and stick securely with strips of gummed brown paper or sellotape. Insert small gifts. Cut two 4-foot lengths of the crêpe paper, lay these on top of each other (one thickness of cover looks mean) and wrap carefully round the cylinder, crimping the ends close to the card each side and tying with string, then ribbon. With scissors zigzag the ends of the wrapper. Paste a band of gold foil round each end and paste stickers over the cracker itself. (A larger Santa figure cut from a card would be more in scale if you have one to hand.) Lay down the centre of the table.

Womble and Disney Place Cards

Children do love place cards, and Womble or Disney characters are always popular. Drawing and painting them from examples to hand shouldn't be too difficult, even if you are not very skilled with a pen or brush. You could cheat, and buy transfers instead.

Materials

Thin card, white one side (shirt boards again), sharp scissors, acrylic or poster paints, Indian ink, Evostik paper adhesive.

To Make

Pencil card shapes 3–4 inches high. When you have got the portraits right, ink over with Indian ink, and paint them carefully, using bright colours and a small watercolour brush. Write each child's name in the blank space. Cut round with scissors. Lay flat under a tray and a pile of books overnight to press them nice and flat. Should you have any spirit varnish in the house, a quick coat of this will give the cards a dazzling shine. From the same card make small tabs to stand them up with and glue these, after scoring the bend line lightly, into place behind the cards. Make sure the tabs are long enough to hold the card nearly upright.

Gingerbread House

This is a real labour of love and patience but it always creates a sensation at children's parties—'Mummy, there was a little house and we *ate* it'—and will be remembered for years to come. The notion comes from Hansel and Gretel country, of course, and a German friend tells me that the gingerbread house made by her great-grandmother, which was large enough for a child to *get into*, is a treasured family legend. Traditionally, these edible houses were made of proper old fashioned gingerbread, a dry and slightly peppery tasting confection which is an acquired taste, besides being quite difficult to bake. The modern version described here is a cheat, as it is largely constructed of biscuits, sweets and icing sugar, but it looks effective and children will enjoy breaking off chunks to nibble at. Don't be disappointed if the house fails to disappear at a sitting—when all's said and done they are more for marvelling at than eating. 8×5 inches is about the right size for the house—if you make it much smaller it loses impact, and if you make it larger it will take too long and cost a small fortune in materials.

Materials

Packets of smallish oblong biscuits (shortbread, wafer biscuits, etc.) in various flavours and colours to simulate bricks, 1 packet chocolate fingers, 1 lb. cooking chocolate or chocolate chips, 1 lb. icing sugar, lemon juice. Suggested decorations—silver balls, little green trees, Santa Claus (optional), Smarties, hundreds and thousands, chocolate buttons, icing bag (optional).

To Make

Build the house on a large pastry board or breadboard. First make a simple glacé icing as mortar for biscuit bricks. Tip icing sugar into a bowl and add enough lemon juice and/or water, beating vigorously meanwhile, to bring it to a thick creamy consistency. Stand the bowl over a pan of simmering water (or tip into top of double boiler) and stir till it is just warm. Remove from heat. Lightly mark out the rough dimensions of the house on your board, have a pile of unwrapped biscuits and a spatula or knife handy and you are ready to start building. Stick biscuits together with icing to make the foundations, spread a thin layer of icing over the top and stick down a second layer of biscuits, levelling up where necessary with an extra dollop of icing. Continue till you have a box shape about 4 inches high. Now build up the end walls into pointed eaves—these can be 3–4 inches higher than the rest of the house.

The roof is made from two thin sheets of chocolate, stuck down with melted chocolate and decorated with scallops of white icing to suggest tiles (for this you would need an icing bag, or cone). To make chocolate sheets, spread a piece of greaseproof paper on the table and trace out dimensions of the roof sections (approximately 9×6 inches for the size of house suggested) with a pencil. Melt the chocolate carefully till liquid and then spread out flat on the paper with a spatula dipped in water. When set, peel off the paper and use shiny side up. Stick down to biscuit walls with melted chocolate and use more chocolate to join sections together along the top. Decorate with icing sugar tiles, or alternatively, make patterns on roof with silver balls, or Smarties stuck in place with icing as before. After all, it is a fairy-tale house, so it can get away with a touch of fantasy.

Make a front door from several chocolate fingers, standing upright to suggest old timbers. Use more chocolate fingers to outline window shapes and fill in with icing panes on biscuits stuck on flat. Round biscuits can be stuck on to suggest little round windows. Add rows of Smarties, or silver balls, or chocolate buttons to give the outside of the house a nice colourful patchwork look. Spread a thin layer of icing over the pastry board for a snowy garden, using hundreds and thousands for the path. Stick trees here and there, flowerbeds (unseasonal but gay) of Smarties outlined in silver balls, a picket fence of chocolate fingers and anything else that takes your fancy. Then slip the whole works into a large polythene bag and store out of sight till the moment for unveiling arrives.

Making Your Own Presents

There are two good reasons for making your own Christmas presents—one is to save money, the other is to put back some warmth and grace into what seems to have degenerated into a routine gift swap, or worse, cheque swap. When you bestow a gift made with your own hands, skill and time, you give a little of yourself too and *that*, dear readers, is what transforms the Christmas share-out into a gesture warming the hearts of giver and receiver alike.

Which is not to say that it is *only* the thought that counts. The thought that goes into a jumper two sizes too big (bound to fit if I make it on the large side), in an unbecoming colour (cheap line) and unfashionable style (it will keep her *warm*, that's the main thing) is probably, at its tangled roots, more a wish to punish than to please. Similarly, cobbling a loop of tape to the corner of a felt square and passing this off as a pot holder suggests the conceited belief that any old rubbish should be good enough for friends and relations if it comes from you.

No, hand-made gifts can be cheap, quickly made, but they should be attractive, if possible useful, neatly and carefully put together and finished with a craftsmanlike attention to detail. The one prescription I trust when it comes to present giving is not to give anything away you wouldn't be pleased to *get*.

Size—literally and metaphorically—matters much less than we tend to imagine. Slight but imaginative presents—prettily papered notebook, painted box full of pins or paperclips, hand-cut stencil—often give more genuine pleasure than elaborate Presents with a capital P, which leave the recipients feeling obligated, uneasy and faintly resentful. Between friends, I think this is the mark to aim at. With intimates there is usually no problem choosing an appropriate present—you know their tastes, lacks and enthusiasms. I hope the following section of the book will provide ideas for presents you would enjoy making and they will enjoy getting. When a doubt arises—you haven't seen her for years—rather than make a desperate guess as to what she may *not* have, why not give her a really super *de luxe* version of something she almost certainly does have—beribboned bath cap, say, even an elegant little needlecase, with chamois leather pages, silk cord trimming and embroidered initials. A trifle, yes, but a luxurious trifle. In cases of grave doubt, you really can't go wrong with a present of food—see Home-made Hampers.

On the practical side, leave yourself a reasonable length of time for planning, buying materials and making. Most of the present ideas which follow are quite quick to make, but collecting together all the tools and materials may take a couple of expeditions and it is much pleasanter to set about it serenely, with time to spare, than dash about in a last-minute flap. Some of the most imaginative present-givers I know fix on one line, as it were, each Christmas (punched belts one year, engraved glass mugs another) and give all their friends and relations variations on the same theme. This is a sensible policy in many ways—you only need one set of tools and materials, you get skilled and deft through practice and repetition, and there are no invidious comparisons to be made. On the other hand, doing the same thing over and over again strikes some people as plain torture. It comes down to a question of temperament—so decide first which yours is.

Fun Jewellery

Most girls aged between seven and seventy are pleased by a bit of feminine frippery at Christmas time. Here is a selection of ideas to make yourself, ranging from jokey Mickey Mouse pendants for small fry, to glamorous gilded pendants for the more sophisticated lady. Buy the findings (trade name for clasps, clips, etc.) from one of the stores who do a mail order service, listed in the Suppliers' Index.

Papier-mâché Pendants

If you are making papier-mâché Christmas tree ornaments, save some of the pulp (see instructions for pulp making under Christmas Tree Ornaments) to make up into brightly painted pendants hung from leather thongs. These make excellent presents for the seven to seventeen age group.

Ideas for papier-mâché pendants

Materials

Papier-mâché pulp (a jam jar full makes approximately 1 dozen pendants), Polyfilla or Wallart (art shops, craft shops), fine wire or gilt wire rings (Suppliers' Index), poster or acrylic paints, gold spray paint, Indian ink, one medium paint brush, one sable brush for fine detail, polyurethane varnish (ironmongers, paint shops) or Humbrol clear enamel (hobby shops, art shops). Leather thonging to hang the pendants from can be found at craft shops and some trimmings counters in big department stores. Allow about ¾ yard per pendant. Use silk embroidery twist or thread for finger knotting cord.

To Make

Roll out the pulp thinly—about ¼ inch—on smooth surface with a rolling pin or milk bottle. Cut into heart shapes, Mickey Mouse heads or roughly circular shapes to paint sun faces on (see illustrations). Slip the cut-outs on to a piece of cooking foil and bake in a moderate oven till dry and hard. Trim off ragged edges with a sharp knife. Coat both sides with Polyfilla or Wallart, smoothing with a damp knife and working the plaster well into cracks, dents, etc. Take some trouble over this because a really smooth surface will take paint better and look twice as professional. Put the shapes back into a low oven and bake till dry. Sand all over till smooth and flat. Touch up any cracks and flaws with more Polyfilla or Wallart and bake again. When dry, pierce holes at the top of the pendants with a large darning needle tapped through with a hammer. Thread wire loops, or gilt wire rings (Suppliers' Index) through the holes. Now give all the pendants a coat of white undercoat, front and back. You may need to do this in two operations, depending how neat-fingered you are. Suspend from an improvised washing line to dry—a length of wire tied round two bottles will do the trick. The pendants are now ready to paint. Use quick-drying acrylic or poster paints, and fine sable brushes for the decoration. Gold spray paint is useful for adding a bit of shiny detail quickly—a gold heart with painted decoration in green, red and white looks festive and pretty. Use Indian ink and a sable brush for painting in outlines. It goes on more smoothly than black paint and allows you to draw in fine detail easily—like the features on the sun faces.

Anyone with a bit of painting experience will probably have their own ideas on how to decorate these pendants, but for complete beginners, here is a breakdown of how I did mine.

Mickey Mouse Heads

Mickey's face is delightfully quick to do, using Indian ink on white undercoat. Copy the face on to a Mickey cut-out, roughing it in very lightly with coloured chalk or charcoal as a guide if you are nervous of launching straight in with indelible ink. (Chalk or charcoal is better than pencil, which is hard to get off again.) Paint the back of his head solid black with the ink. Add a bright red bow-tie for a spot of colour. Let the ink dry for a minute or two, then varnish by dipping the pendant into a pot of polyurethane varnish, or clear lacquer. Hold it by the ring, and let the surplus varnish or lacquer drip off into the tin. Suspend over the drying line again till quite dry and hard. Don't let two pendants touch each other at this stage, because they will stick firmly together and will be difficult to part without damaging one or both. Thread a red leather thong through the gilt loop.

Note. An even quicker way to turn out Disney pendants would be to make plain white round papier-mâché discs and decorate them with Disney transfers. Varnish these too to protect the transfers.

Hearts

These look prettiest decorated in a folk-art style. (See illustrations for ideas.) The base colour can be anything you like—red seems right, but black, green and gold all look pretty. Give the shapes two coats of the base colour, front and back, for good coverage. When quite dry, paint on the designs with sable brushes and paint colours used in a thick enough solution to give crisp outlines and solid colour. You will find some colours give the right effect in one go, others may need touching up. It's a good idea to try out the white 'flicks' on a piece of paper first, as it takes a little practice to brush them in quickly and confidently. Varnish as above. Alternatively, brush on Humbrol clear enamel for a brilliant shine. Use a soft brush. Thread on leather thongs, or chains.

Sun Faces

These were inspired by old prints of the Inca sun god. They lend themselves to slightly more sophisticated colour schemes. I painted some in black and white and gold on a terracotta background; others in black, with touches of vermilion, on a bright yellow base. Either way it helps to rough in the rays and features very lightly first with a stick of charcoal which washes off readily (art shops). Paint in the features with Indian ink, using the tip of a very fine sable brush and a light touch. This needs breath control and a steady hand, but it's quite easy—have a practice run on a piece of paper. Paint in the terracotta background, between the rays, *after* you have painted the sun face. For terracotta, give one coat of Indian red, then another of crimson for a touch of depth. With gold paint touch in the centre line of the sun rays. Don't worry if a white film forms on the gold paint, this vanishes when the pendant is varnished. The yellow sun can have some of his rays picked out in vermilion. Give his cheeks a ruddy glow by washing on a watery solution of vermilion. Varnish as above. Thread on thongs, chains or silk cords. You can make cord yourself by finger knitting embroidery silks (see page 81).

Gilded Shells, Acorns for Pendants or Earrings

Gold leaf transforms pretty natural objects into regal-looking pendants to hang on gilt wire chokers (I used small scallop shells and acorns, but you will be able to think of many more). A pair of matched shells can be made into earrings to complete the set. Unless you are very pushed for time, don't cheat by using gold spray paint. I have tried both, and compared the results, and there is no getting away from the fact that gold leaf looks twice as rich, mellow and magnificent. Transfer gold leaf costs no more, in fact probably less as there is no waste, and it is much easier to apply than you might suppose—not much more difficult than applying ordinary transfers. You can buy proper gold leaf or Dutch metal, which is slightly cheaper and not quite so yellow, in booklets of about twenty sheets from a good artists' supply shop. The same shop will supply you with writers' gold size to stick it on with (the leaf and size are generally bought for gilded sign writing) I have used PVA adhesive instead of the size, with excellent results. You also need acrylic paint in Venetian red, as a base for the gold. This counterfeits the red clay underlay used by traditional gilders, and means that any flaws in your gilding will show up as flecks of warm red, which looks even prettier than plain bright gold.

Before gilding you will need to drill holes in the shell pendants, and assemble acorn and shell earrings.

Materials

Acorns or prettily shaped small shells (scallop, cockle or mussel shells are all suitable; use a larger one for a pendant, two small ones of the same size for earrings), ear clips, gilt wire rings, gilt wire chokers (Suppliers' Index), transfer gold leaf or Dutch metal (artists' supply shops), writer's gold size (artists' supply shops) or PVA adhesive, small tube acrylic paint in Venetian red, medium paint brush, hand drill plus masonry bit in a fine size—darning needle thickness—lump of plasticine, Araldite adhesive and Polyfilla.

To Drill Shells

Wedge the shell, concave side up, into a lump of plasticine. Drill slowly with a very fine bit—the size of a large darning needle—inserted into a hand-operated drill. Your hole will be piercing the thickest part of the shell, at the top, so this may take a minute or two. Don't rush at it or you may shatter the shell. Thread a gilt wire loop through the hole.

Shell Earrings

For these you will need gilt clips with a flat base to stick the shells to (see Suppliers' Index). Araldite adhesive is the strongest for the purpose, and you can also use it mixed up with a little Polyfilla as a filler for the shell. Most shells will need a little filling inside to provide a surface to stick the ear clips. For this, warm the two tubes of Araldite in the oven for a few minutes, mix together as instructed on a tiny piece of glass or paper, and work a little Polyfilla into the adhesive until it is of a pliable, though sticky, dough-like consistency. Use methylated spirits to clean the Araldite off fingers, tools, etc. Now scoop up a little of this filler and level off the inside of the shell with it. Don't fill up the entire shell, because that may make it too heavy to wear, just enough to give the clip something to grip on. Leave the shells a good 48 hours for the filler to set hard. Then coat the clips with Araldite and press into place on the filler. Stand something on top to weight them and leave to dry hard.

Acorn Pendants

Nothing very tricky here. Cement acorn and cap together with Araldite and insert a small brass screw eye into the top of the nut. A screw eye with gilt loop is best as it will let the acorn hang properly from a wire choker. (Gilt wire chokers cost approximately 25p each. Don't use any other sort of wire because it leaves a curious tidemark round the wearer's neck.)

Gilding

First paint the shells, or acorns, all over (inside the shells as well as outside) with Venetian red. Give two coats for good cover. When perfectly dry, brush on a thin coat of writer's size or PVA wherever you want gilding—outside of shells, all over acorns. Follow maker's instructions for size. With PVA leave till the milky adhesive becomes clear. Then take up a sheet of transfer gold leaf and press the shiny side firmly over the tacky surface of the object, smoothing with the fingers till the tissue backing shows a bare patch where the gold leaf has come off on the shell or nut. Touch up any blank spots where the gold didn't stick by pressing on another scrap of leaf in the same way. If it won't stick you may need to dab on a spot more PVA and re-gild as before. Tiny flaws don't matter, as I have explained already. Smooth down the gilded surfaces lightly with a scrap of silk and set aside to dry thoroughly. Then brush gently but firmly in one direction with a soft brush, to bring up the fine detail like the grooves on a shell and the pitted surface of an acorn cap. Finish off the pieces and protect the gold by brushing on a thin coat of varnish.

Masai Watch

One of the most attractive and original beadwork trinkets I have seen recently was a Masai 'watch' brought back by a friend from an African holiday. Real watches are a status symbol the Masai can rarely afford, so their womenfolk conjure up these charming beaded 'watch' bracelets instead. I was especially captivated by the inspired use of old metal zipper teeth to suggest minute signs. They are not difficult to copy, and they would make a lot of impact worn on suntanned wrists come summer.

Materials

A selection of small china beads in the following colours: white, red, green, orange, blue, old metal zipper, a small piece of leather to make the base of the bracelets, glover's needle, fine needle for beading, button thread.

Beaded Masai watch

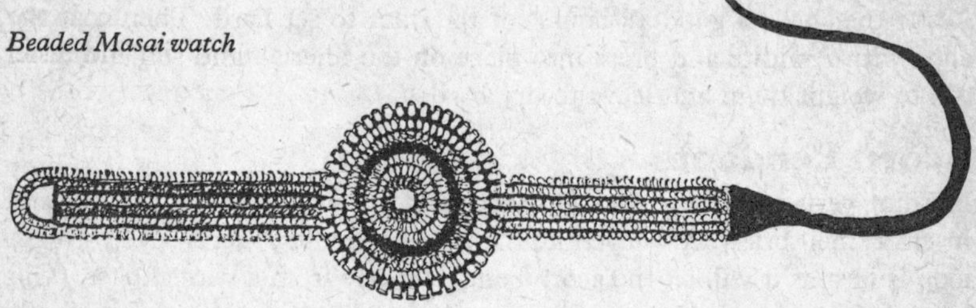

To Make

The beads should be sewn to leather that is sturdy but not too thick to pierce with a needle. (The Masai use cowhide cured with cow's urine but there's no need to push authenticity too far.) Draw the button thread (or linen thread, but it *must* be strong) over a cake of beeswax before use to strengthen it and help prevent it snarling up as you work.

Use an ordinary watch and strap to cut a pattern. Make the 'watch' face on the large side—$1\frac{1}{4}$–$1\frac{1}{2}$ inches in diameter—and the strap, which is cut in one with the face, slightly over $\frac{1}{2}$ inch wide. Scale all measurements

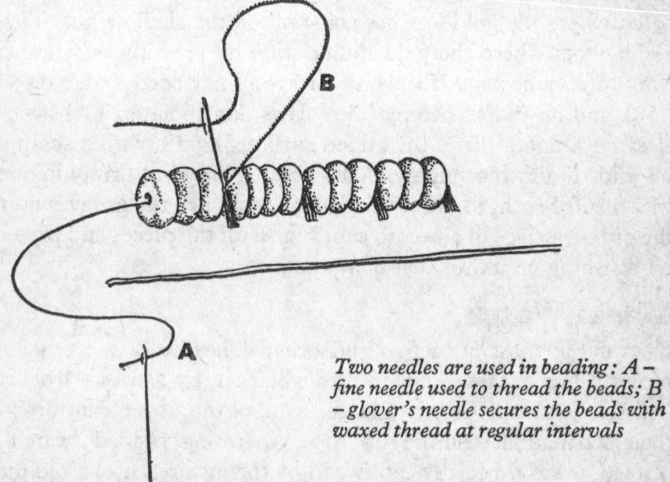

Two needles are used in beading: A – fine needle used to thread the beads; B – glover's needle secures the beads with waxed thread at regular intervals

up a little for a man. The length of the strap doesn't matter because it is adjustable. Cut the leather base out with a sharp knife. Begin beading the watch face in the centre. The Masai use a flat bead, but a small flat button would do. Stitch this down securely. The beading is done with two needles threaded with separate lengths of thread. The fine needle takes up beads, three or four at a time, while the glover's needle is used to catch these down to the leather base at regular intervals (see diagram). Only the glover's needle stitches through the leather base. This sounds more complicated than it is in practice. An alternative method some people might find easier, would be to thread the beads on fine wire, catching this down with the glover's needle and waxed thread. Either way, build up the beaded 'face' with ring after ring of coloured beads (the Masai use white for the centre bead then red, green, orange, blue, white, and red, working outwards). Leave a narrow strip of leather ($\frac{1}{8}$ inch) all round the face for the zip teeth. Cut the fabric part of the zip away close to the teeth and snip off a piece long enough to encircle the watch face. Then stitch down all round, with the teeth pointing outwards, taking the stitch over every third gap between the teeth. Finally, bead the strap lengthways, leaving out the narrow leather tie at one end. The Masai use green, red, white, blue and orange for the strap, in that order, reversing it for the other half. Continue the beads round the little cut-out loop at the end of the strap. To fasten, pull the tie through the loop and knot.

Beads, Buttons, Nuts and Washers

Fashion jewellery makes use of the most surprising ingredients these days. One good-looking chunky necklace I saw recently was made up, on closer

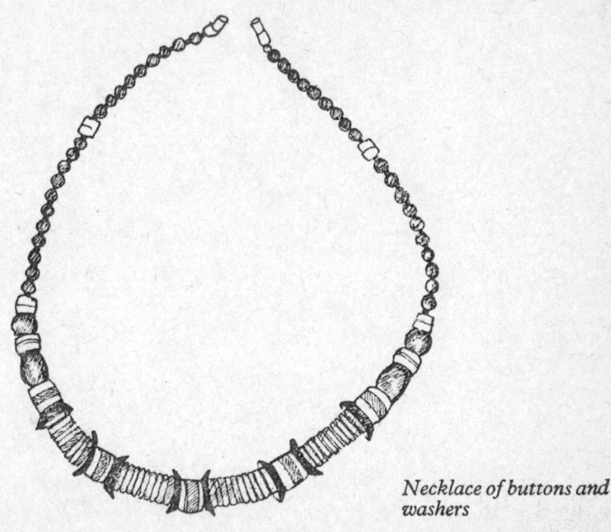

Necklace of buttons and washers

inspection, almost entirely of very ordinary buttons—plastic shirt and fly buttons—interspersed with short cylinders of polished brass, reminiscent of some of the bits and bobs which plumbers carry around with them on repair jobs. A quick visit to the nearest brass fittings suppliers, plus a trip to a button counter, together with a few wooden beads and the usual findings—nylon thread, clasps—would supply you with materials for several smashing necklaces at very small cost. Keep an open mind as to the brass pieces you choose—you could use brass nuts or washers, or small cylinders normally used to link two sections of narrow piping together—anything shiny, neatly finished, with a hole through it. Each necklace requires approximately (depending on the width of the brass pieces) 36 small shirt buttons in a tawny shade, 8 small brown fly or trouser buttons, 24 wooden beads, including some oval ones and as many brass pieces as look right and make up a necklace that sits comfortably round the base of the neck. (See illustration for how to arrange them for best effect.) Thread the necklace on two lengths of nylon thread for strength, passing them as one through the beads, but through opposite holes of the buttons. Knot the ends of the nylon threads very securely to the clasps, using a reef knot, then push the loose ends down inside the first few beads. Once you have made a prototype you should be able to turn out a necklace like this in a quarter of an hour.

Note. Old pearl buttons look particularly pretty threaded together—if you can get hold of any.

Me, Me, Me, Mine

Everyone likes to have his initials on things, even where they cannot ordinarily be seen. It gives a small, harmless thrill of self-importance—a fact DIY-givers can usefully capitalise on. A routine gift becomes quite special when emblazoned with someone's initials or name. Here are a few ways of playing the name game.

Embroidery

Hand-embroidered initials or monograms give considerable uplift to most items of clothing—shirts, T-shirts, sweaters, ties, scarves. They are invariably embroidered in satin stitch, a simple over and over stitch which anyone at all acquainted with a needle can master rapidly. The style of initial varies with the type of garment. Plain angular capitals are most

Diamond monogram

suitable for men's shirts, where the custom-made touch is to have a tiny pair of initials in a contrasting colour worked just above the heart region. Ties and scarves require something bolder, a diamond-shaped monogram perhaps (see illustrations). Unless you are very sure of your man's tastes, stick to discreet, unemphatic colours for monograms. A girl's shirt gets a fashionably 30s detail with a large monogram worked on the breast pocket. White on black silk looks glamorous. T-shirts can take bolder treatment, both in the lettering and colour contrast. Sweaters can be worked with initials in cheerfully contrasting colours, on a pocket, high up on one shoulder, or in the centre of a short tight sleeve. Other possibilities include pyjamas, knitted gloves, towels, even a humdrum face flannel. The only item I wouldn't bother with is that classic venue for initials—the pocket handkerchief. Who uses them nowadays?

Initial worked in satin stitch on embroidery frame

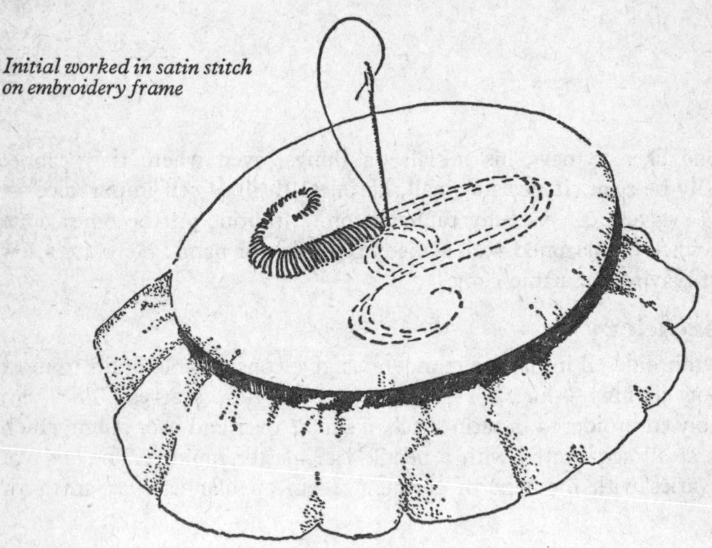

Method

The method is the same in all cases, closely worked satin stitch over a padding of plain running stitch. The rule is to use a thread which matches the article in question—cotton on cotton, silk on silk, etc. Use fine thread or wool for neatness. A small embroidery frame over which to stretch the fabric helps to get even satin stitches tight (see illustration), but I have worked initials successfully without one. When initialling a pocket you might find it easier to unpick the pocket, then stitch it back on after the embroidery is done. In the case of a ready-made tie, you can work a little pad of tissue paper up inside the tie to provide a cushion. If the paper gets caught up it can be pulled away carefully afterwards. When embroidering woollen garments don't pull the stitches so tight that you pucker the garment.

Note. Wash your hands punctiliously before stitching garments that cannot easily be washed.

Knitting

If you are knitting someone a sweater for Christmas incorporate their initials in a brightly contrasting colour. This is quite simple provided you are working in a straightforward stitch—stocking, moss, etc. Decide where initials would look most decorative—on a hip pocket, sleeve, or yoke. Draw them out to the size and shape you want, keeping to simple letter outlines. Transfer the shapes to squared paper, counting one square per knitting stitch. Then simply knit in the requisite number of stitches as you come to them, carrying over the main wool of the sweater behind as with any knitted insertion.

Printing

One would have to be very blasé not to be impressed by a scarf, tie, or T-shirt printed with one's own initials. The letters can be applied as an overall design element—you've seen those *haute couture* accessories printed all over with the initials of the presiding genius—or combined in various ways with tie-and-dye patterns. For beginners, simple potato cuts used with fabric printing inks are probably the best way to stamp initials on fabric. Potato cuts give a slightly soft-edged print which combines particularly well with muzzy tie-and-dye effects.

Materials

Fabric printing inks and thinner, piece of thick felt for printing pads, large potato, sharp knife or gouge for cutting out design, small tins or jars to mix inks in, paraffin for cleaning up.

To Make

A printing pad (one for each colour) can be improvised from a square of felt laid on a cushion of newspaper. Squeeze inks from tubes into the jars and tins, and add some thinner in the proportions specified by the maker (usually one level dessertspoon to 2 inches of ink), mix well, then spread over the printing pad till evenly coated. To make the potato stamp cut a large potato in half, wipe it on a cloth, and draw the initial letters on the cut surface with a felt pen. Cut round the letters to a depth of about ⅜ inch with the penknife point, then carefully cut away surrounding potato so that the letters are left in relief. You may have to do two or three cuts to get clear, shapely outlines. Before launching on the fabric itself practise prints on a piece of newspaper. If the print is fuzzy, the ink is too thin. Add more tube ink to the mixed solution and re-ink the pad. Wipe the potato from time to time to remove starchy liquid. Re-ink the potato between each print, and re-ink the pad whenever it becomes dry. The dye pads can be kept moist overnight by covering them with several sheets of wet newspaper. Leave printed fabric to dry overnight, or longer in the case of black. Fabrics printed by this method can be washed in the usual way, but should not be rubbed too forcefully or boiled.

Engraving on Glass

One girl I know had the bright idea of giving various children of her acquaintance inexpensive glass mugs inscribed with their names for Christmas. Children are always delighted to have something unmistakably their own, especially in a large family where so many things have to be shared. Mugs and tumblers can all be decorated in this way. Look for sturdy shapes in reasonably thick glass.

Materials

Mugs or tumblers, glass engraving tool.

To Make

The easiest way to engrave accurately is to print the name or initials clearly on a piece of white paper and fix this in place inside the tumbler or mug with Bostik or sellotape. (You can write directly on to the glass with a felt pen, but this is liable to rub off as you work.) If you mistrust your skill at lettering, use Letraset transfer type to make up the design. The name or initials can be enclosed in a decorative frame.

Personal designs for pottery and glass

Painting

There are special paints for use on china, pottery or glass which stand up well to daily washing and drying. (See Home-made Hamper for details.) Work out designs and any decorative flourishes beforehand on paper, then copy onto the chosen surface with a felt pen. A child's mug and bowl will be twice as popular inscribed with his name and some simple decoration.

Crochet and Sewing

Mohair Shawl with a Scalloped Border

As heating becomes more expensive, voluminous shawls to snuggle into are bound to grow even more popular. This one is crocheted from mohair wool in a pretty openwork stitch which covers the ground at great speed. There is a lot of ground to cover, because the shawl is large enough to wrap the average female from head to foot. It is delightfully warm, light as a sigh. and takes only 8 ounces of Pingouin Volutes or similar mohair wool. Use largest hook size 1.

To Make

The shawl is worked in Godot stitch.

Abbreviations: ch.—chain; tr.—treble; dc.—double crochet.

Start by making a chain 100 inches long. Row 1: 1 chain, 1 double crochet into the next stitch, * 1 ch., 1 dc. into each of the next 3 sts, 2 ch., 1 dc. into each of the next 3 sts *, 1 ch., 2 dc., 3 ch., turn.

Row 2 and following rows: * (* 2 tr., 1 ch., 2 tr.) into 2 chain space, (1 tr., 2 ch., 1 tr.) into 1 ch. space *. End each row by making half a motif, i.e. if the last space on previous row is 2 chains, make 2 trebles in the space and then turn with 4 chains, if the last space is a 1 chain space, make 1 treble into this and then turn with 4 chains; and continue in the next complete pattern, so that each row is 2 half patterns shorter than the previous row.

Continue like this till there is just enough space for one complete pattern. Complete that and finish off. Rejoin wool at foundation chain and make 4 chains, then make 6 double trebles into each space and 2 chains wherever there is not a space, so you end up with a fairly closely worked frill all round the shawl.

Mob Cap and Dorothy Bag in Printed Cotton

There is nothing wrong with practical gifts if they can be pretty too. Make a mob cap and dorothy bag (for curlers or make up) from the prettiest flowered lawn or cotton you can find, trim them with ribbon or lace and line with plastic for practicality, and you will have a present to take the chill off getting up on a cold wintry morning.

Mob cap in printed cotton

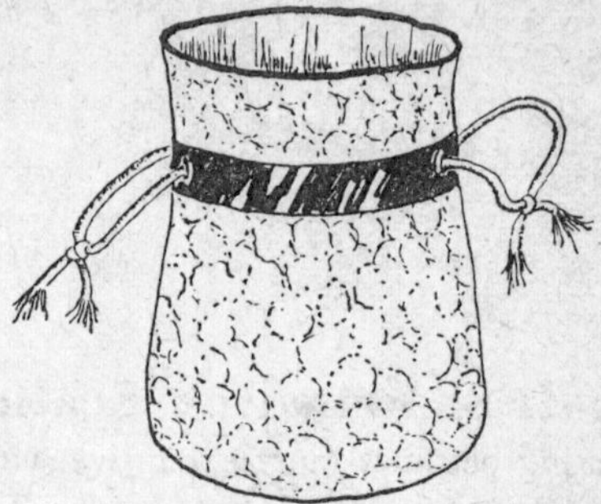

Dorothy bag

Materials

¾ yard of 36-inch-wide lawn or fine cotton, same amount of lightweight plain coloured plastic, 3½ yards of ¾-inch-wide grosgrain or satin ribbon to tone with flowered lawn, 1½ yards of fine cord, ½ yard of narrow elastic, bias binding, sewing thread.

To Make

Lay lawn and plastic on top of each other and cut circles A and B, and rectangle C as shown in the diagram, cutting both materials as one.

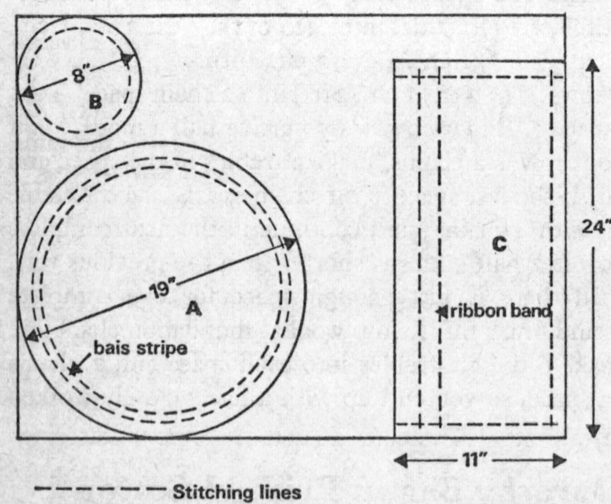

Layout for cap and bag

Cap

Circle A makes the mob cap. First bind the circumference of the cap with ribbon. Fold ribbon in half and tack round over the raw edges, easing it slightly as you go. Then machine with matching thread close to the ribbon edge. Pin or tack a circle of bias binding 1 inch from the outer edge, as shown by the dotted line in the diagram, and machine down both sides of the binding with matching thread—matching the fabric this time. Run narrow elastic through the bias circle and draw the cap up to fit an average head size. Stitch the ends of the elastic together firmly.

If you prefer a lace edging, fold in $\frac{1}{4}$ inch all round fabric and plastic circles, and machine. Then machine lace down on top, stitching close to the edge of the lace.

You can finish off the cap with a ribbon bow stitched at some point to the gathered elastic channel seam.

Dorothy Bag

With right sides together, stitch side seams—separately this time—of lawn and plastic rectangle C, as shown by dotted lines on diagram. You now have two tubes. Pin lawn circle B to one end of lawn tube, as shown in the diagram, tack round, then machine, press seams open and turn right way round. Do the same with the plastic circle B and plastic tube. Turn this seam side out. Slip plastic bag inside lawn bag. Cut a length of ribbon which will encircle the top of the bag, as shown by dotted line on C. Stitch the ends of ribbon together to make a ribbon ring. Cut four small round holes in the ring, opposite each other, as shown in the illustration, and buttonhole these closely (these are for the cords to pass through). Pin the ribbon circle in place round the bag, tack and machine down both sides, close to the ribbon edges. Cut length of fine cord in two and thread through the ribbon, from opposite sides of the bag, to make two loops that draw the bag shut. Knot the ends of the cords. Bind the top of the bag in the same way as you bound the mob cap, with folded ribbon stitched down all the way round.

Quilted Caftan

I can't think of a nicer present for a young grand-daughter or niece than a quilted cotton caftan, to wear on the way to bed, around the house or down to the beach in summer. The traditional caftan, snug and close fitting round the top and flaring widely round the hem—many of them are open at the sides for greater freedom of movement—is one of the most flattering, comfortable garments ever created. It is also, like many traditional garments, easy to cut and sew, as most of the sections are simple rectangles and all the seams are straight. The three measurements required are the shoulder width, neck circumference, and neck to ankle length. With these you will find it quite simple to work out your own pattern from the accompanying diagram. The yardage required will be twice the neck to ankle measurement. I suggest you make the caftan up in a washable quilted cotton—one of the small Provençale-type prints on a dark ground would look pretty bound in contrasting cotton bias or braid.

Materials

Quilted cotton material, matching thread, two cards cotton bias, coloured rick-rack (optional).

Caftan layout

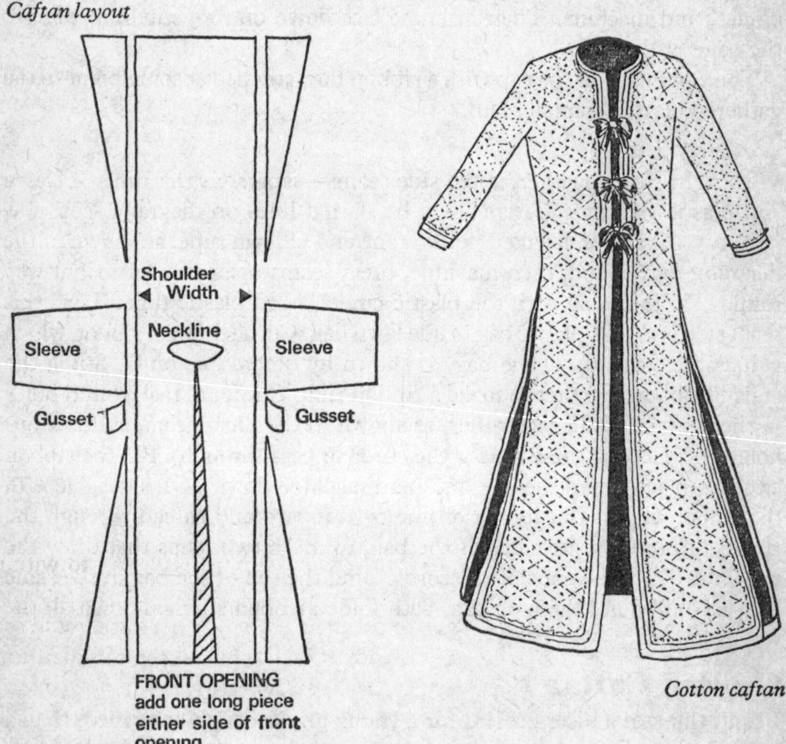

Cotton caftan

To Make

As you will see from the diagram, the caftan consists of a long narrow rectangle based on the shoulder width and neck to ankle measurement, slit up the middle to the halfway mark. To this are sewn long tapering triangles to add width at the hem, and smaller rectangles for the sleeves. Under-arm gussets give ease of movement and a close fit round the

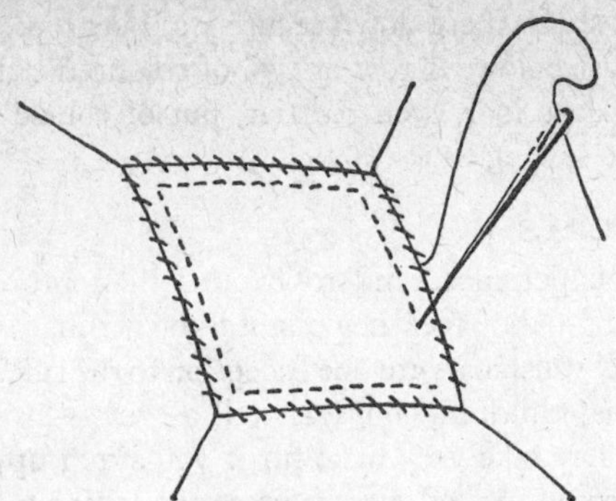

Sewing under-arm gusset

shoulders and bust. The caftan front has four triangular pieces added, the back two. The side triangles form a point just above the waist, and graduate from nothing at the apex to around 4 inches at the base. The triangles either side of the front opening are narrower at the base (2–3 inches) and begin at the same height on caftans for small, flat-chested girls. On older girls, with the beginnings of a bosom, these extra pieces are added just below the neckline, tapering out gradually from there, to give extra width across the bust. The accompanying diagram should clarify all these points. Use run and fell for all the caftan seams, because this makes for strength and neatness. I machine up the run seam, and hem the fell one down by hand. This way, no machining is visible on the outside. Trim seam allowances away where possible too, otherwise the padding will make them bulky.

I found the best order in which to join up the pieces was like this: run and fell sleeves to centre strip matching ▲ signs at shoulders. Then run and fell triangular pieces either side of back and both fronts. Now run and fell sleeve seams; I taper seams slightly towards the wrist first, to within 1½–2 inches (depending on the size of the caftan and girl) of shoulder seam. A diamond-shaped gusset approximately 2½×2½ inches large will be inserted here. But first run and fell the side seams, from a point a few inches below the apex of the triangular side pieces to a point 1½–2 inches below the shoulder seam. This will leave you with a diamond-shaped hole under each arm. Cut a diamond piece large enough to cover this, allowing ½ inch extra for seams, and insert this by hand, hemming round with tiny stitches as if inserting a straightforward patch. Now all that remains is to round out the neck slit a little as shown by the dotted lines in the diagram; and stitch braid or binding right round all the unfinished edges of the caftan. For front fastenings either use braid or binding loops and covered buttons, or more authentically make three sets of ties from the bias or braid and stitch these down securely at bust level, just above waist level and again just below. A row or two of coloured rick-rack, machined down all round, does look even prettier, but of course it bumps up the cost as well as the sewing time.

Fur Waistcoats

Children in my experience tend to be less than properly grateful for presents of clothing—they feel they ought to be getting sweaters and suchlike anyway. Furry waistcoats are one exception to the rule. Perhaps because they are luxurious, children—boys as well as girls—love them and wear them to death. They take very little fur if you stitch up oddments into a patchwork. You could use leftovers from re-modelling a coat of your own, or buy a bag of sheepskin pieces in bright colours for a pound from a mail order firm in Scotland (see Suppliers' Index). Buy a simple jerkin or waistcoat pattern, or cut your own, using a child's shirt or dress bodice as a guide. The shape couldn't be simpler for a flat-chested child (see illustration). The only points to watch out for are the armholes—make them large, to accommodate jerseys—and the neckline, which should be set away from the child's neck, otherwise there is a tendency for the garment to bind uncomfortably. Line the waistcoat with scraps of woollen material such as flannel, and bind the edges and seams with wool or cotton braid, or strips of soft leather.

Fur waistcoat

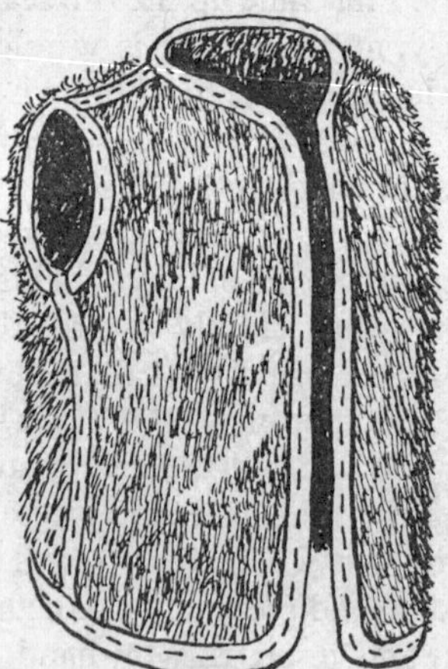

To Make

First cut the pattern, if you are making your own. Don't leave seam allowances, or turnings. Stitch the fur oddments together to make pieces large enough for the back and fronts of the waistcoat. Lay the pieces flat on the pattern to work out the best arrangement. Try to keep the fur pile running the same way. Trim the pieces to regular shapes to make them easier to sew. If you have a machine which does zigzag stitch, you can use this to join the pieces together from the back. Otherwise stitch them together by hand, using a glover's needle (to prevent the stitches ripping the hide), button thread and two lines of overstitch, going up one way, then back the other, like cross stitch when opened out flat. Don't pull too tight, and push the fur down inside with the needle, otherwise you will get into a mess. When you have completed the back and front pieces, lay them fur side down, place the pattern shapes on top, chalk round them and cut away any extra with a sharp knife or razor blade rather than scissors. Cut lining pieces the same size, plus ½-inch seam allowances at shoulders and side seams. Machine these and press open. Join the three fur sections together by stitching braid or leather strips down sides and across shoulders as shown in the illustration. Do this by hand if the fur is shaggy. Fit the lining inside. A few dabs of Copydex to catch the lining and waistcoat together will make the next stage easier. Use clothes pegs or paper clips to hold fur and lining together round outer edges and armholes. Then hand stitch or machine braid or leather binding all round. Waistcoats like these don't really need fastenings, but you can add these if you wish. Ties made from doubled strips of leather or braid would look right. Stitch these inside the waistcoat fronts, oversewing securely to the lining.

Silk Ties

However scruffy they may look much of the time, most boys—I am thinking of the eight to fourteen age group—like to be able to slip into something slightly more elegant for special occasions. One friend with several boys of various ages tells me that their best ever Christmas presents were simple straight ties, in silk, and stunning colours, which an imaginative friend doled out a year or two back. A really simple idea to copy, and economical too, as one yard of silk 36 inches wide will make at least a dozen ties. Get a really good silk, preferably a rough, raw silk which looks rich and expensive even whittled down to a narrow ribbon of a tie. It might be an idea to buy a yard of white or natural silk and tie-dye it (nothing dyes so splendidly as silk) in an accordion pleat method for broken stripes.

To Make

If you are going to tie-dye, do this before making up the ties. Accordion pleat the silk across from selvedge to selvedge (so the stripes run across the ties), keeping the pleats uniform in width and fairly narrow—¾ inch. Then tie with string, thread and nylon string (different types of tie will give stripes of varying distinctness and character) at intervals along the pleated length. Dye, following maker's instructions, using Dylon hot water dye for the best results. You might find one dye gives enough colour and pattern—a pink or blue dye with white broken stripes where the ties are removed would look very dishy. For more colour and variety, tie with more string and re-dye a second colour. Suggested colour combinations are yellow, then coral or pink; light blue, then mid green; snuff brown, then light purple.

To make the ties, cut or tear the silk lengthways into narrow strips—2½ to 3 inches wide. With right sides together, machine raw edges to make a long tube. Open out seam and iron flat. Tack across one end (to give you something to push against) and turn right side out with a ruler or pencil. Press again under a damp cloth so the seam runs along the middle. Fray the ends to ½ inch depth.

Tie-dyed Silk Squares

Anyone with do-it-yourself inclinations will almost certainly have played about with tie-and-dye so I will not waste time expatiating on the delights and rewards of this fascinating pastime. One technique you may not have come across, however, is the method of folding squares to give precise square-within-square patterns. Worth passing on as it gives silk or cotton scarves an impressively professional look, plus the usual tie-and-dye

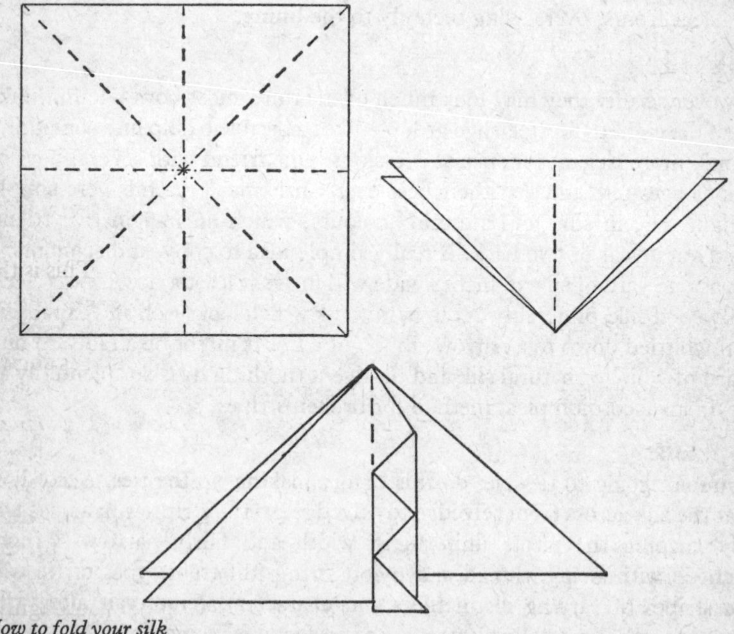

How to fold your silk

characteristics of richly shaded colours and soft-edged patterns. A soft pure silk or cotton lawn would make elegant squares to tie peasant fashion, or knot round a shirt collar. Or cut costs by using cheesecloth, which dyes beautifully and is still one of the cheapest materials around. For maximum colour interest and variety start with white or natural cloth, then tie-and-dye in two stages. For speed, and sharper definition, start with a square of silk or cotton in a good plain colour, tie-and-dye it a stronger, darker colour. Dye pale blue green or brown, for instance, or a red silk, black.

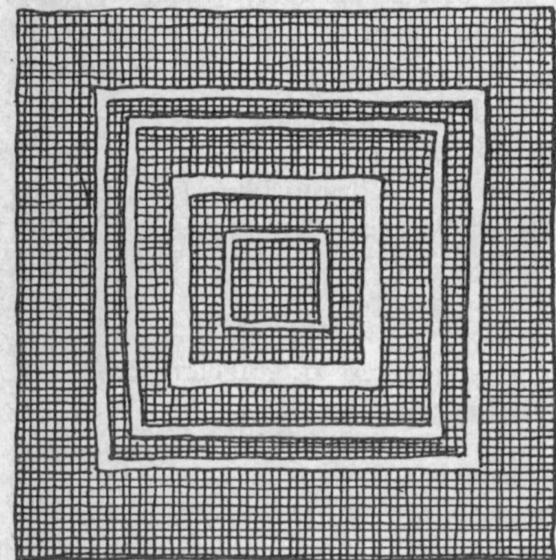

The tie-dye effect

To Make

The squares must be *square* for the folding to come out right. Fold and crease the square to make the familiar Union Jack pattern shown in fig. 1. Then, pinching up the exact centre spot, arrange the square, using the creases, to give the pyramidal shape in fig. 2. Now with pins or chalk mark off regular intervals along the base of the pyramid on both sides. This is the only tricky part of the operation. The number of marked spots depends on the width of the square, and the bulkiness of the material. Using the marked spots, fold each corner of the pyramid inwards towards the centre as shown in fig. 3. Pin down to keep the folds in place while you fold the other three corners in the same way. If your measuring and folding has been accurate the zigzag folds should meet up in the middle—this is important because it means the tied square patterns will meet up accurately in the corners. Now begin tying the folded bundle from the centre point downwards, removing pins as you go. Each tie will produce a square pattern on the finished scarf. Dye with Dylon hot water dye, following maker's instructions carefully. Leave the ties on while you rinse the scarf out thoroughly. When the water runs clear, remove ties and rinse again. Dry flat if possible.

Iron carefully. Make rolled hems all round the square. Loosely woven materials are best hemmed before dyeing.

Baby's Sleeping Bag

A present for which any new mother would be grateful is a baby's sleeping bag. They are expensive items to buy, and an extra one always comes in useful. This one is designed to come on and off easily, with a drawstring neckline and zip at the tail end. When the baby outgrows the bag, it would be a simple matter to remove the bag part at the foot, leaving a warm nightie. With this in mind I chose a warm pure wool doctor's flannel. It comes in a smashing bright red, or pretty creamy white. Bind the neck and cuffs in ribbon and appliqué a design—the apple shown here is a nice easy shape to do—at the foot where the baby can see it. (You can buy ready made appliqués which only need to be hemmed into place.) The whole thing takes just 1 yard of material. It will fit a baby from three months to one year.

Materials

1 yard doctor's flannel, 12-inch zip, matching thread, gingham scraps for appliqué, 1 yard ribbon binding, 1 yard narrow tape.

To Make

Using the squared pattern here as a guide, draw out the pattern pieces on a large sheet of brown paper. The bag does not have to fit anywhere so don't take great pains to get the measurements mathematically accurate. The raglan shoulder seams are the only important ones. I suggest you cut out the sleeves first, then lay these in place, as shown by the dotted lines on the pattern, to get the size and shape right, remembering to allow ½ inch for shoulder seams on the bag itself. (This allowance is included in the pattern measurements throughout.) Use french seams or, better still, run and fell throughout, for strength and comfort. Those with fancy sewing machines can use the seam finishing stitch instead.

Sew up sleeve seams. Insert sleeves into armholes, tacking them into position before machining. Stitch centre back seam of sleeping bag, leaving 3 inches open at the top for the neck opening. Stitch the two tail pieces to the zip fastener, one each side, to make an oval-shaped inset. Then tack this into place at the foot of the garment, so that the zip runs across from side to side. Fold ribbon binding in half and tack round neckline and cuffs. Machine. Thread narrow tape drawstrings through the ribbon bindings and stitch down at the halfway mark to prevent them slipping out in the wash. Tack appliqué shape into position as shown, and hem down all round with tiny stitches. Work stem in satin stitch in a suitable colour.

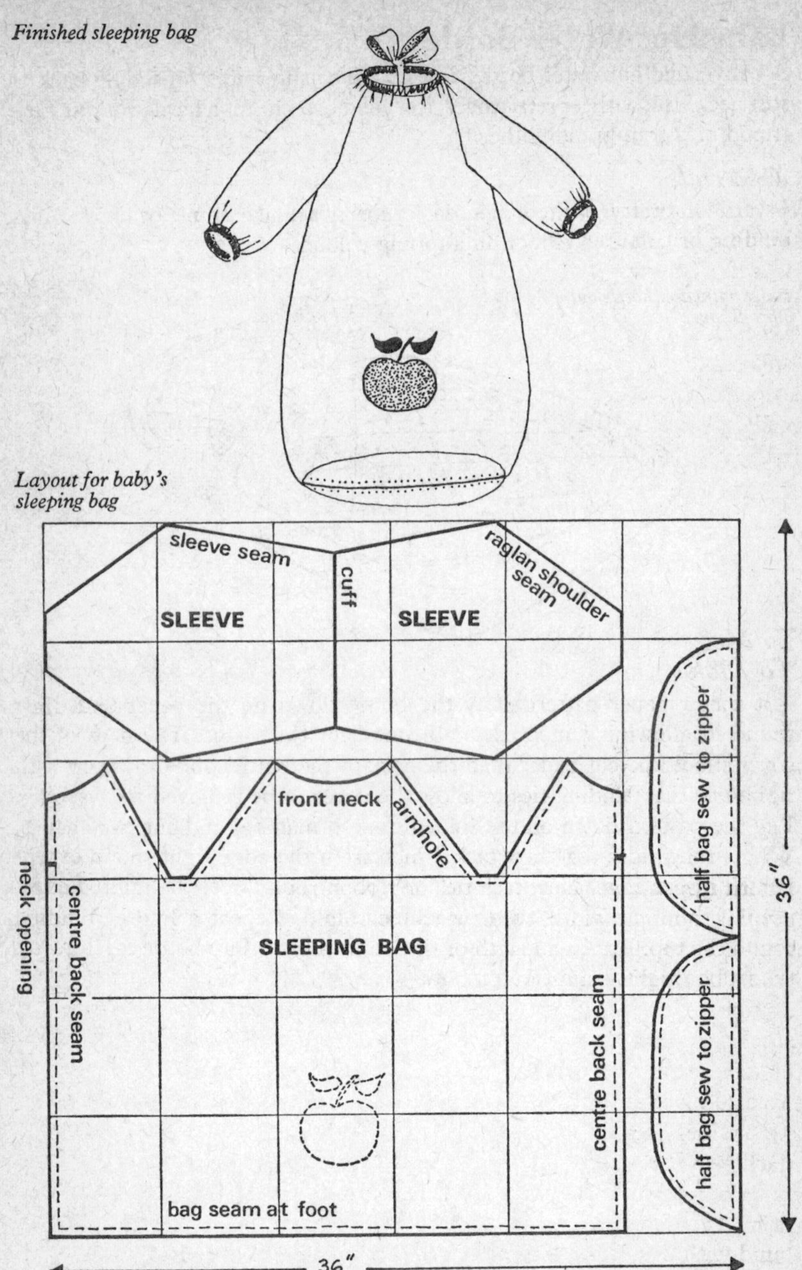

Finished sleeping bag

Layout for baby's sleeping bag

Baby Hot Water Bottle

A baby-sized hot water bottle is just right to slip under an aching back or stiff neck and, with a pretty cover, is a good present for a hard-working girlfriend or a frail grandmother.

Materials

¼ yard of pretty quilted material (Liberty's make some beauties), bias binding or coloured ribbon in a toning colour.

Baby hot water bottle with quilted cover

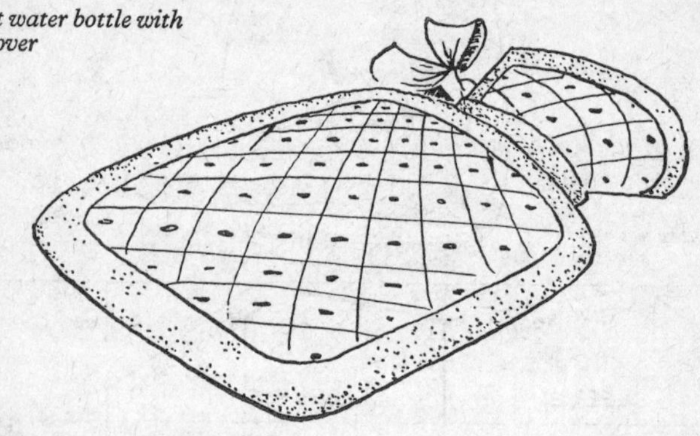

To Make

Cut a newspaper pattern. Lay the bottle down on the paper and draw round it, allowing ½ inch extra all round for the seams. The neck of the cover should be cut wider than the neck of the bottle, and drawn up with ribbon or bias binding ties to allow the cover to be removed for washing. Lay the pattern down on the folded quilted material and cut two shapes. With wrong sides together, tack ¼ inch from the edge right round except for the upper edge. Now tack ties or ribbon round over the quilted edge, keeping binding width even. Machine round. Repeat a line of binding round the top. Attach a length of ribbon as shown. Slip bottle in, draw up the ribbon tightly and tie in a bow.

Re-Cycling

Now that everyone has become so waste-conscious it is almost a moral duty to think of ways to use up odds and ends around the house—cast-off clothes, scraps left over from dressmaking activities, odd balls of wool, even plastic containers and tins. There is no reason why these shouldn't be re-cycled into attractive and acceptable gifts with the help of a little imagination, and some bright trimmings. Here are a few ideas to start you off.

Soft Toys from Felted Sweaters

Old sweaters washed and shrunk till they feel like felt can be used to make attractive soft toys, which small children invariably prefer to the most elegant dolls. The more felted the better, as these are less likely to unravel.

Humpty Dumpty made from felted sweaters

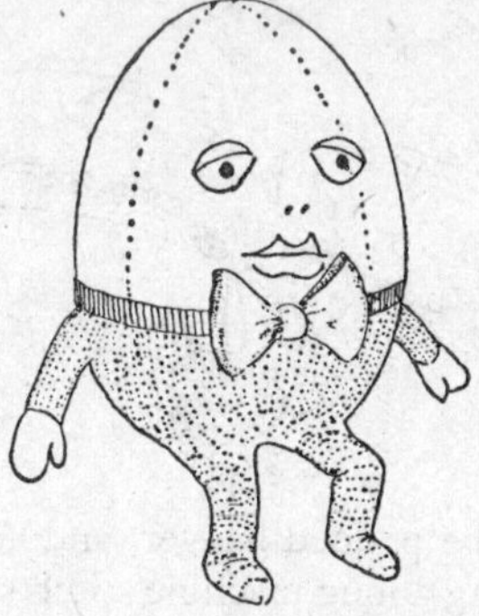

Choose a simple pattern, without too many pieces or small gussets—Humpty Dumpty is a current favourite—and buttonhole or oversew each cut-out piece before stitching the toy together. This can be done by machine—using loose tension and a thread with some give in it—or by hand. Stuff with kapok, embroider features, etc. in contrasting wool, and make any little extras such as hats or waistcoats in scraps of bright felt.

Odd Scraps of Leather

Use leather to jazz up a pair of knitted gloves (see illustration). The gloves should be plain, preferably in a dark colour (knitters can make their own, non-knitters should buy them at stores specialising in school outfitting) and the leather cut-outs, which can be as bright as you like, should be appliquéd to the *backs* by hand, with a glover's needle and buttonhole

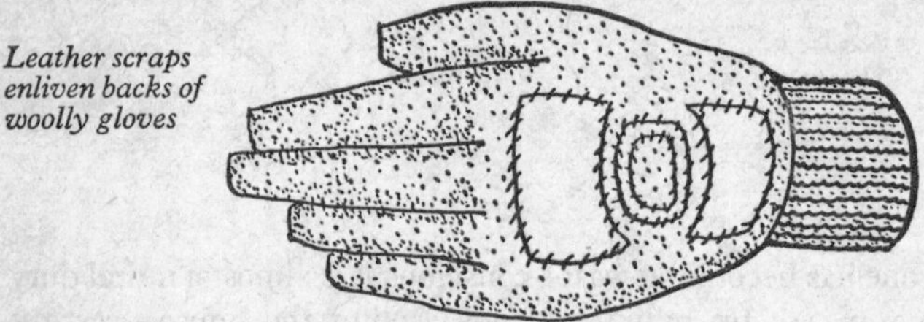

Leather scraps enliven backs of woolly gloves

thread. Use a straightforward over and over stitch and don't pull the thread too tight or the glove will not give properly.

Fabric Scraps

Pretty scraps can be used to dress up a set of padded hangers to add a touch of luxury to any woman's wardrobe. Woolworth's sell cheap wooden hangers—it's usually as well to cut an inch or so off each end because modern clothes tend to be cut very narrow across the shoulders. Use cotton wadding to pad the hangers, glueing the paper side down and binding round lightly with cotton. To make the covers cut fabric strips wide

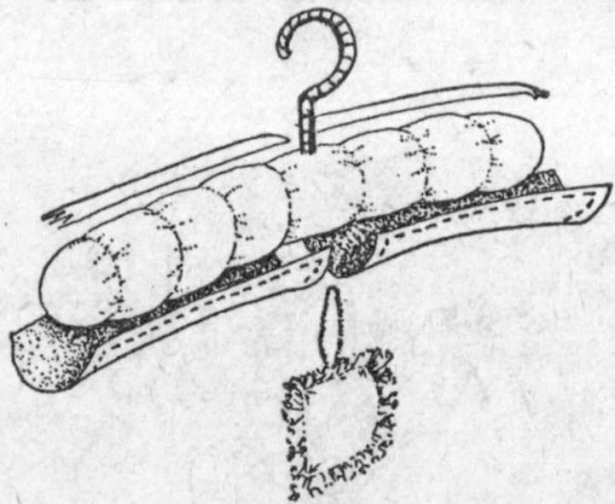

Coathanger cover made from two sausages of scrap material

enough to meet round the padded hanger, and allow 1 inch extra for the seam (see diagram). Using a long machine stitch sew the strips, right sides together, into two long sausages—one for each half of the hanger. Draw up the stitching, turn the sausages right side out and ease into place over the padding. Bind the metal hook with bias binding or a long strip of the same fabric cut on the cross. Catch the cover in place in the middle and tie a ribbon bow. You can hang a lavender bag from the ribbon if you want to be really swanky.

Small Bright Oddments of Closely Woven Cotton or Wool

Make these into pretty pincushions for home-dressmaking friends. In the old days pincushions were stuffed with sand or bran (pet shops), which helped to keep needles and pins sharp. Plump little heart shapes trimmed with silk cord look attractively Victorian. (Make your own cord by finger knitting embroidery silk—see caption to diagram.) Add a ribbon loop to hang the cushion by, and a Christmas greeting spelt out in pins. Complete the set by making a matching needlebook—an invaluable sewing accessory, this. Glue fabric over a strip of light cardboard for the needlebook cover, trim with cord to match the pincushion, and make the 'pages' out of any light soft woollen fabric or chamois leather cut out with pinking shears. Stitch the 'pages' to the spine of the cover with a few large stitches in strong thread—the cord will hide the stitches.

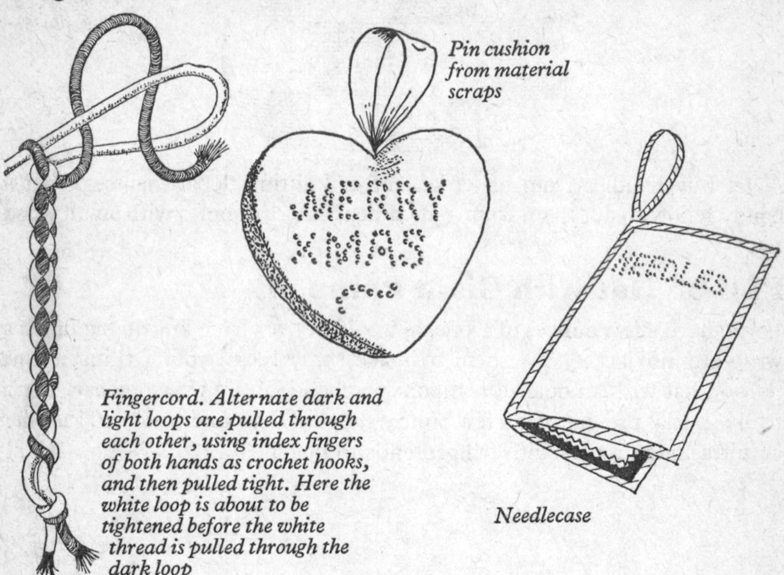

Pin cushion from material scraps

Fingercord. Alternate dark and light loops are pulled through each other, using index fingers of both hands as crochet hooks, and then pulled tight. Here the white loop is about to be tightened before the white thread is pulled through the dark loop

Needlecase

Oddments of Knitting Wool

Nothing looks gayer than a patchwork of knitted squares in bright colours. If you do not have enough to make a blanket or shawl, catch up on the trend for soft bags with wooden handles—the kind traditionally sold for knitting bags. Stitch together enough knitted squares—they should be roughly the same size and weight, finer wool can be knitted up double—make a rectangular pouch 10 to 12 inches deep and slightly wider than the handles. Make a bright cotton lining the same size as the knitted pouch. Stitch to handles with strong thread, easing the knitted bag and lining as you go along to give a pouchy effect. If you have a spare piece of soft leather or suède you could cover the handles with leather, saddle stitched into place all round (see illustration). To get a really tight fit, wet the leather (not suède, which is stretchy enough already) and stretch and mould it round the handles before stitching. Use a glover's needle and buttonhole thread passed over a cake of wax to stitch with. Waxing strengthens the thread and the glover's needle helps prevent the leather tearing at the stitch holes.

Patchwork bag made of knitted squares

Note. Buy handles from haberdashery or knitting departments, or get a handy fellow to cut them from $\frac{3}{8}$ inch deal and drill holes with small wood bit.

Pull-on Hat with Giant Pompom

If you have a few ounces of Donegal wool left over from knitting yourself a wrap-around jacket, use them to make some lucky young thing a chic pull-on hat with an outsize pompom perched jauntily over one ear. For a really special present, get a few ounces more of the same wool and knit her an ultra-long muffler with fringed ends to match.

Pompom hat

Materials

3 (1 oz.) balls Paton Four Seasons in Donegal 5407, or similar Donegal wool. Pair each Nos. 9 and 11 Milwards Disc needles.

Tension: 6 sts and 8 rows to an inch over stocking stitch on No. 9 needles.

Abbreviations: m.1p. means pick up horizontal loop lying before next stitch and purl into back of it.

With No. 11 needles cast on 108 sts, and work 14 rows k. 1, p. 1 rib, decreasing 1 st. at each end of last row: 106 sts.

Change to No. 9 needles.

Next row: * p. 3, m.1p.; rep. from * to last 4 sts, p. 4: 140 sts.

Starting with a k. row, work in stocking stitch until hat measures 5 inches from start, ending with a p. row.

Shape crown as follows: 1st row: (k. 8, k. 2 tog.) 14 times: 126 sts. 2nd and every alternate row: purl. 3rd row: (k. 7, k. 2 tog.) 14 times: 112 sts. Continue decreasing in this way on every alternate row till you have worked the row (k. 1, k. 2 tog.) 14 times. Next row: purl. Next row: (k. 2 tog.) 14 times. Next row purl. Next row: (k. 2 tog.) 7 times. Thread yarn through remaining 7 sts, draw up and fasten off securely.

Pompom

Cut two cardboard circles as shown in the diagram. Wind wool round closely till the centre is almost filled up and you have to thread wool through with a darner. (The pompom must be fat and bushy, or the hat loses half its charm.) At this point, cut round outer edge of discs with sharp

Making the pompom

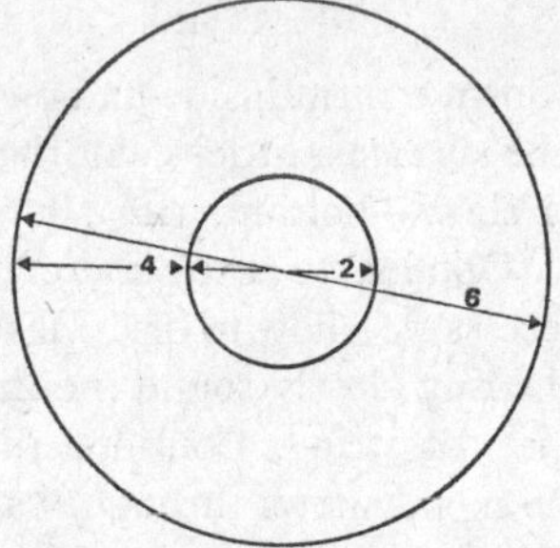

pointed scissors to slice through all wool loops. Part discs a little, twist wool round several times and draw up tight. Remove discs. Clip pompom with scissors to make a perfect ball.

To Make Up

Press hat lightly on wrong side using cool iron and dry cloth, omitting ribbing. Join seam. Stitch pompom securely to one side close to edge.

Tins

Yes, tins, the kind paint, food and pastilles come in, can be smartened up and given a new lease of life in all sorts of directions. You will find other suggestions for making more of tins scattered through the book. The ideas outlined here are for quickly-made small presents. Remember that it's the little craftsmanly touch that makes the difference between a pleasing and useful thing and a candidate for the White Elephant Stall.

Tin into String Holder

Sturdy medium-sized tins with lids—like cocoa tins—make smart string dispensers if you cover them with string. Any string will do. Rough twine in its own natural colour looks very chic if you stick it down with glue size, which gives a subtle sheen. Or combine different coloured strings in stripes of varying widths. Or use plain white string and paint it the same colour as the tin.

String holder – a tin covered in string

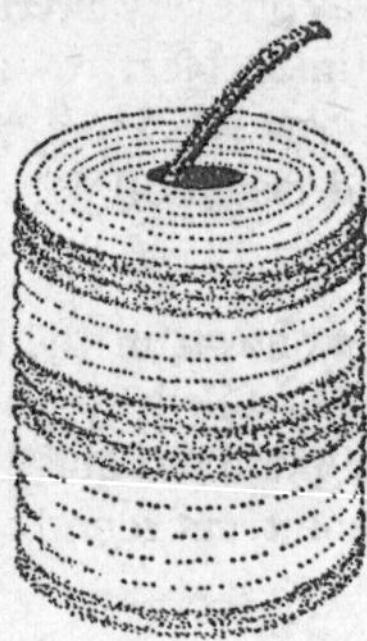

Soak off labels. Rub down the tin inside and out with wire wool or fine sandpaper to roughen the surface a little. Paint the inside and the parts of the outside which will show—bottom, rims, underneath the lid—with Humbrol enamel paint. (Obtainable at toy and craft shops.) Allow to dry. Give a second coat if necessary. Allow to dry. Make up some glue size in a thickish solution. Wind string closely round the tin, tucking the loose end under the first few twists of string. Continue till the tin is completely covered, making sure no metal shows through. Paint over the string with size till well saturated. Push the other loose end under the string binding with a small screwdriver—the size will hold it in place. Leave to dry. Punch a hole in the centre of the lid with a large nail. Sand with emery paper to smooth the edges, or better still use a needle file if you have one. Alternatively, hammer a brass eyelet into the hole. To cover the lid, dip a length of string into the size, which will make it tacky enough to stick to itself, and coil carefully round on top, leaving the string hole clear, of course.

Pin Boxes

Small sturdy tins with hinged lids make useful pin boxes. They look attractive if you give them a coat of metal primer and follow up with two coats of scarlet enamel, rubbed down between for an extra smooth finish. Use Letraset transfer type to print PINS elegantly on the lid, and finish with two coats of clear varnish, rubbing down lightly with a damp cloth sprinkled with a little Vim in between each coat.

Decorated pin tin

Another way of decorating them would be to punch the letters and a simple border pattern before painting. (See Punched Tin Tree Ornaments.)
Note. It would be a kind thought to fill the tin with pins. This idea can be used for other small items: paper clips, elastic bands, stamps.

Desk Set

More tins—the 2 gallon paint size this time—plus oddments of hessian, webbing, leather and cardboard add up to a very good looking desk set which would gratify anybody who works at home. Use ordinary jute sacking (a pet food shop might be able to let you have some empty sacks) bound with twine and leather for an expensive hand-made Italian look.

After some thought I settled on a big waste bin, a small pen and pencil

Desk set from painted tins, sacking, string and cardboard

holder, and a covered folder as the most useful items for the modern desk. Not many people use ink, so they don't need blotters these days. My folder was a good size for storing letters, but people whose work involves plans or drawings would be grateful for an outsize folder—say 2 feet by 1 foot 6 inches—large enough to hold all their work in progress.

Materials

2 gallon paint tin, 1 pint paint tin, 1 sheet mounting board or heavy cardboard, 2 sacks, rough twine, scraps of brown leather, 1 yard striped webbing, 2 sheets brown paper, glue size, Stanley knife.

To Make

First clean out the tins. They are to be covered inside and out so you need not remove every scrap of paint. Remove thick encrustations with a scraper, especially round the top. Really thickly crusted tins can be cleaned off by soaking in a strong caustic solution for 48 hours, scrubbing now and then to help the acid to its work.

Warning. Add caustic to water in an enamel or galvanised bucket, not the other way round. Avoid splashing. Wear rubber gloves. Don't let small children anywhere near bucket or contents. Use old scrubbing brush. Clean the tins by rinsing with cold running water and finally swabbing with weak vinegar water to neutralise the acid.

Waste Bin

A 2 gallon paint tin makes a capacious waste bin. I trimmed the top of mine with leather, and bound stripes of twine round the outside. These hold the sacking cover taut as it dries as well as looking very handsome. I lined the bin with ordinary brown paper, but you could use brown felt, or a plain, dark vinyl-finished wall paper.

First paper the bin inside and out with brown paper stuck on with glue size. The paper inside acts as a lining, outside as a backing to the sacking, which is so loosely woven the metal would show through otherwise. Bring the paper lining up as high as the overhanging rim at the top. Cover the bottom of the inside too. Use plenty of glue size as it will give the paper a dirt resistant finish that can be wiped over when dry. Cut a length of sacking long enough to roll round the tin, with ½ inch extra each side. It should reach from just below the top rim to the bottom rim of the tin, plus 1 inch to fold under the tin all round (see diagram). Coat outside of tin and sacking cover liberally with size. Bring top edge of measured sacking cover up to meet the top rim of the tin. Trim wildly fraying edges back a bit but do not fold frayed edges under because they will be covered by the leather binding. Smooth the cover over the tin, trying to keep the grain of the fabric vertical right round. Draw the bottom edge down over the bottom rim. Make a neat join down the side where the two sacking edges meet as follows: fray edges back so that the woven edges just meet. Tuck frayed edges under on both sides (fraying the edges makes for a less bumpy join). Brush on lots more size and press flat with your fingers. Now, using rough twine, bind a stripe 1 inch deep round the top and bottom of the tin, starting ½ inch or so in from the rim. Add a third stripe halfway up the tin. Coat the twine liberally with size as you go. (Sticky job this, but it pays off, so persevere.) To finish off twine binding, fray out ½ inch or so and push this under the last twist with a penknife blade. Leave it all to dry out thoroughly.

Now for the leather binding round the top rim. This isn't difficult to do, but you will need a very sharp knife for trimming the leather. First pack out the depression round the rim with a length of piping cord, sash cord or clothes line. Saturate with size and push down into the depression. This will give the leather edge a smooth rounded look. Cut a strip of leather long enough to encircle the tin, and 1½ inches wide. Don't worry if you have to join it, but do leave ½ inch overlap at join. Turn leather strip face down on a sheet of glass or other scratch-proof surface. Using a sharp knife blade (it is possible to do this with a razor blade wrapped one side with sticky plaster, but this requires care and practice) pare away the back of the leather strip along the edge to give near paper-thinness. The technical term for this is skyving, and it gives a smooth, professional finish, as well as near invisible joins where two sections of leather overlap (see diagram). Joins should be cut on the slant, like bias binding, and the edges both sides skyved carefully so that there is no ridge where they overlap. You will need a little practice to skyve accurately. Use a spare bit of leather to work out the proper angle for cutting, and the amount of pressure you need to taper the edge without cutting right through it. Now try out the leather strip binding to check it for size. Wetting it makes it more malleable still, and easier to smooth into place round the rim. Damp it both sides with a sponge. Now coat with glue size and smooth carefully round the rim of the tin, checking to make sure the outer edge is level. Press under the overhanging rim inside to give a smooth finish. Thc leather will be very stretchy, and size is not an impact adhesive, so you have time to fiddle about getting everything just right. Leave to dry out. You will find the leather binding dries taut and smooth and looks very professional. Cover the base of the tin with a circle of felt or paper.

Pen and Pencil Holder

Make this in exactly the same way as the bin, using a much smaller tin. I used a 1 pint paint tin, but any sturdy well-shaped tin would do.

Covered Folder

Measure out and draw the outline of the folder on mounting card. A narrow spine is essential as it means the folder will accommodate far more letters, papers, etc. Score lightly each side of the ruled spine with the point of a Stanley knife and bend like a book cover. Now using the card cover as a pattern, drawn the outline on the sacking with a felt pen, allowing 1 inch foldback all round. Cut out with scissors. Brush glue size over cardboard and sacking and stretch the sacking into place over the card, pulling it taut over the edges and glueing down the foldbacks inside. Make sure the sacking is drawn really smooth and tight, with the weave vertical to the folder edge throughout (the weave is so pronounced with sacking that any deviation from the straight leaps to the eye). Trim sacking off at corners of folder and these will be covered with scraps of leather. Make leather corners as shown in diagram, skyving all edges and overlaps for neatness. Damp and glue as above.

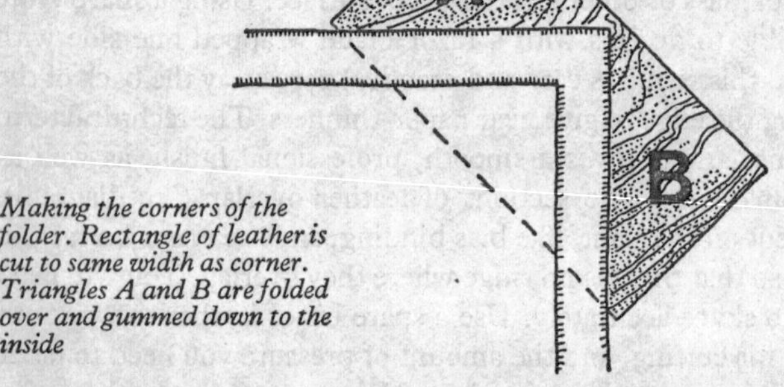

Making the corners of the folder. Rectangle of leather is cut to same width as corner. Triangles A and B are folded over and gummed down to the inside

While the cover is drying, make a brown paper covered cardboard lining for the folder. If you paste the paper lining down directly over the sacking foldbacks you will get a bumpy, amateurish finish inside. Instead, cut two rectangles of light cardboard 11 × 9¼ inches. Cover with brown paper cut ½ inch bigger all round and folded back and stuck down. You now have two neatly papered panels which fit inside the folder covers. Cut two squares of light wadding material, or more sacking, to glue into the spaces left inside each cover, to level them off. Then paste a strip of brown paper over the inside of the spine, and glue the papered panels into position either side of the spine. Glue webbing round the middle of the folder to give a belted effect. You can emphasise this by stitching a buckle one side and making brass eyelets in the other. More simply, oversew the ends to stop them fraying and knot loosely.

Old Bottles into New Vases, Tumblers, etc.

The notion of converting those old wine bottles into simple, chunky vases and tumblers to give away as presents must appeal to anyone with a practical mind. Now, there are patent bottle cutters which are efficient but not cheap considering the simplicity of the components. By all means invest in one if you are the kind of person who feels happier with tried and tested equipment and an instruction sheet printed in six languages. True do-it-yourselfers, however, may be interested to know that they can save themselves a couple of pounds, and get as good results using a standard glass cutter (Woolworth's, ironmongers) and a little ingenuity.

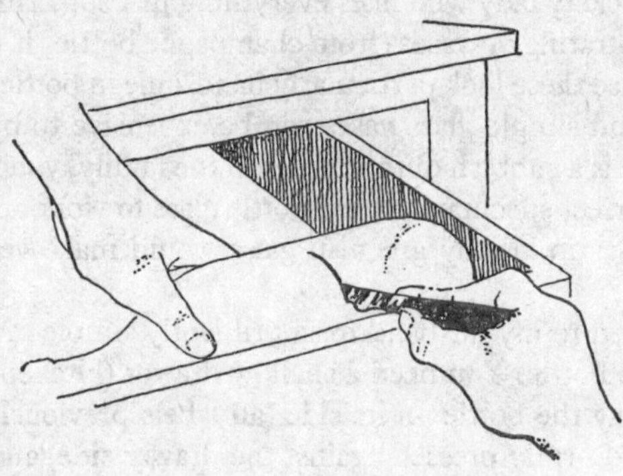

Scoring the glass

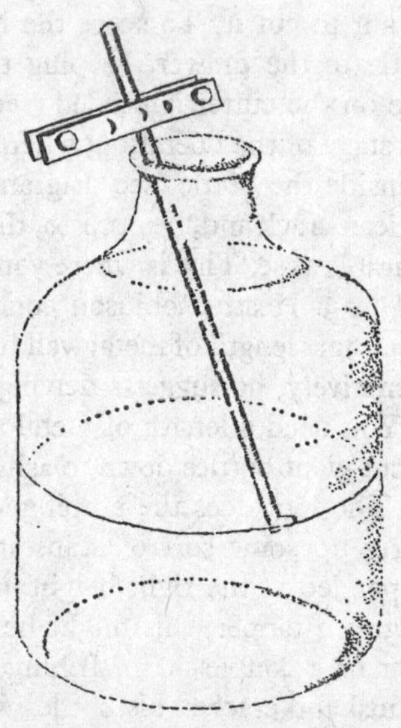

Tapping the top part of the bottle free

One point I should emphasise before going into details is that bottle cutting is somewhat chancy whatever tools you use because mass-produced bottles often have weak spots or flaws which can develop into cracks as you cut and tap the glass. So be prepared to discard a good few of the bottles you operate on. Collect empty sherry, port and champagne bottles for preference because these tend to be made of thicker, stronger glass. And don't expect the results to be absolutely symmetrical and of uniform thickness because the chances are that your tumblers and vases will be a little thicker at one side than the other and not perfectly round. This makes them all the more appealing to some tastes, but might be a reason for not giving a set to a pernickety lady who likes everything just so. If in doubt, I would suggest concentrating on vases (from champagne bottles if you can get hold of some) because these look particularly handsome in bottle glass, the shape is just right, and simple glass vases can be expensive to buy. One further point—if there is a rubbish dump digger in the family, you might be able to get some imperfect specimens of old bottle glass to work on. Some of those Victorian bottles in cloudy greenish glass would make very pretty vases, tumblers, etc.

I am indebted to my husband for a brilliantly simple method of scoring evenly round a bottle. You need a shallow drawer (kitchen table type) and glass cutter. Lay the bottle on its side (all labels previously soaked off) in the drawer, end firmly pressed against the drawer side, and rest the cutter on the front of the drawer with the cutting edge touching the bottle at whatever point you want to cut it. To score the bottle evenly all round, simply rotate the bottle in the drawer, keeping the cutter hand steady. Only a gentle pressure on the cutter is needed (see diagram 1).

Now for the second stage of the operation, where a sharp tapping round the scored line from inside the bottle (see diagram 2) induces the scored line to become a nice clean crack and, hey presto, the bottle top lifts off and you are left with a desirable vase. This is where you need a little ingenuity. My husband knocked up a Heath Robinson contraption from a sewing machine foot wired to a short length of metal wall bracketing which did the job successfully. Alternatively, he suggests delving into a Meccano set, if you have one handy. You need a length of metal about 8 inches long (or longer if you want to cut giant bottles down to ashtray size) bent up into a little foot at one end. The foot does the tapping, of course. It helps considerably if you can rig up some sort of adjustable washer to keep the tapping appliance suspended at the right height in the bottle. Depending on what you are using as a tapper, this might be a thick rubber washer slipped on like a collar or a couple of small hinges bolted together with screws and nuts. My husband cracked his bottles without resorting to any of these refinements, so don't let the lack of a washer put you off.

As you tap round inside the bottle a faint frosted line will appear along the groove, a sign that the glass is cracking right through. If any *vertical* cracks appear, you will just have to abandon the bottle and begin again. When you have completed the circuit, remove the tapper and gently pull the bottle in two—it should fall apart. The rim will need grinding down with carborundum paper—first medium, then fine grade—to make it perfectly smooth. Do this by laying the paper flat on the table and rotating the glass rim on it, exerting firm and even pressure. A vase rim doesn't have to be quite so immaculate as a tumbler. Tumblers are more comfortable to drink out of if you bevel the rim slightly. Do this by folding over a strip of abrasive paper and circling the rim with it, pinching it hard between the fingers.

Note. Clear glass can be decorated with names, initials, or patterns scratched on with a diamond stylus or painted with Deka colour. (See Suppliers' Index.)

Plastic Container into Watering Can

This is my own contribution to the re-cycling effort (I daresay thousands of people have independently had the same brainwave but I haven't met them) and I am rather proud of it. It neatly fills a long-felt lack in my household for a small light watering can to deal with indoor plants. All you need is one of those small plastic cans with handles, and a large needle. To pretty it up as a present, I suggest you paint or spray the container with red or green enamel and stick flower cut-outs (seed packet type) on both sides. Then varnish with polyurethane. One point—the can *must* be complete with screw-top.

To Make

Stick the needle into a cork. Heat the needle over candle flame or gas jet and puncture holes in the screw-cap to counterfeit the standard watering can rose—i.e. rings of holes radiating from the centre. Use a large needle to give good sized holes. Then with a Stanley knife or penknife cut a small triangular piece out of the back of the handle or punch larger holes along the top of the handle. This is to let air in, otherwise the improvised can won't spray efficiently. Wash the can out very thoroughly, to remove any traces of contents. To paint, scrub the outside thoroughly, leave to dry, then paint or spray with brightly coloured glossy enamel (Japlac, paint shops, or cellulose paint sold for touching up car paintwork, garages). It will probably need two coats. Make sure the paint doesn't clog the holes in the screw-cap. Run the needle through to make sure. Stick flower cut-outs on both sides with PVA adhesive (Copydex) and finish off, when

the glue has dried, with an overall coat of clear polyurethane varnish.
Note. Thoughtful present for grandparents with a collection of pot plants, or flat dwellers starting up a windowbox.

Home-Made Hampers

An imaginative selection of home-cooked delicacies, attractively packed, makes a truly regal Christmas offering. In fact, should you ever come up against the problem of what to give those intimidating people-who-have-everything, this is what I would settle for. Arabella Boxer has included lots of suitably elegant and festive items for home-made hampers in her book on *Christmas Food and Drink*, so I won't trespass on her territory here. I'll confine myself to a little general advice.

If you live in the country . . . do include some evocative rural treats such as bramble jelly, quince marmalade, damson cheese. A string of dried wild mushrooms, perhaps. Some jars of dried herbs from the garden—even common thyme smells twice as heady from someone's herb patch as it does from commercial jars. And why not throw in a pretty jar of pot pourri, and a few old-fashioned ribbon-tied lavender bottles (instructions below) to scent their sheets and set them sighing for cottage gardens in mid-summer.

If you live in a town . . . stress exotic and unexpected ingredients or flavouring, the sort of thing that is cheap and plentiful in urban street markets, Indian, Greek or Chinese stores. Roll home-made biscuits in sesame seeds and pine nuts or flavour a rich pâté with a clove of star anise. Look through Middle Eastern cookbooks for recipes featuring ingredients unlikely to reach country friends—preserves made from fresh dates, aubergine pickles, etc.

Having assembled a really mouth-watering list of contents, the containers must come up to scratch or the whole effect will be spoilt. Over the preceding year collect any attractive or unusual bottles and jars (instant coffee jars, stoneware wine bottles, bath salts jars, earthenware mustard pots, Stilton jars). You can buy corks in any size (see Suppliers' Index) for stopper-less bottles and flagons, mustard pots, etc. If you are thinking of sending jams and jellies by post, best collect those honey or jam jars with screw tops—wash and dry carefully before storing away. Small items, herbs for instance, look more appealing if you pack them in the same sized containers, so hang on to glass mustard jars, miniature jam pots or anything else you can build into a set without drastically changing the family's eating habits. Large sweet jars make handsome containers for anything bulky—biscuits, fudge—with the bonus that the recipients can use them afterwards for storing rice, spaghetti, etc. Buy these from local sweet shops. If you ask the proprietor nicely he will probably sell you the big glass screw-top jars for a song, and the non-returnable plastic variety (not so handsome but featherweight, which makes them ideal for posting) he may well give you free. Labels which have been stuck on with PVA adhesive don't soak off readily. Try saturating them with surgical spirit (the nearest easily obtainable thing to pure alcohol) for a few minutes. You will find they can then be removed quite easily. Tins—biscuit, chocolate, nut tins, etc.—need more working over if you want to disguise their original purpose, but you will probably find a few come in handy. The most luxurious container for salted nuts, home-made sweets, would be ahand-painted wooden box. (See Pretty Boxes.) Line with paper doily before filling.

Now for some ways of prettying up your containers to make the most of their delectable contents.

Labels

Pretty stick-on labels decorated with a frieze of holly are just the job for all your glass jars, large and small. The stylised holly borders illustrated are both Victorian, and very decorative. If you are going to make lots of hand-printed labels of the same size, I suggest doing a lino cut. The bolder pattern should be used as a continuous border, but the delicate spray of holly pattern—more difficult to cut into lino—could be used sparingly, perhaps one spray each end of the label. (See Christmas Cards for how to tackle lino cuts.) For the most efficient way to lino print labels see accompanying diagrams. If you plan to print only a small number of labels, or

Holly designs to copy

labels of various sizes, you will probably find it quicker to make a stencil and use this to paint the holly border or sprays. Incidentally, the holly spray was designed without berries, but you could add these by hand for a bit of extra colour. The border is a one-colour design too. It would look attractive printed in unconventional colours—brown, dark red, gold—as well as the more predictable green.

Perfectly plain gummed labels are not all that easy to come by, as I discovered. If you can't get them, use instead sheets of paper from a cheap drawing book and paste them on with Polycell. More trouble, but more classy.

Painted Designs

A really special bottle for really special contents—sloe gin, perhaps—can be turned into something even more special by decorating it with hand-painted designs. Use a medium like Glasfyx designed for painting with oil colours on glass, or the special Deka paints (see Suppliers' Index) which can be baked to near enamel hardness in a domestic oven. Snowflake patterns would be perfect (see illustrations). They are easy to do, extremely pretty, and you only need one paint colour—white. Paint them on at regular intervals over your bottle, using a fine sable brush. Paint the words 'Sloe Gin' on too, if you feel up to lettering, or take the easy way out by printing them on a tie-on label and hanging it round the neck of the bottle.

Snowflake designs

If you would like to tackle a more difficult bit of glass painting, there is a cheating method by which even beginners can get good results. You simply find a coloured design or picture you would like to reproduce, roll it round a pencil and slip it into the bottle. A dab of Polycell on the side of the bottle will hold it in place once you have manoeuvred it into position against the glass. Then all you do is copy the design through the glass. When paint is dry, soak off the picture by filling the bottle with water for a few minutes.

Corks, Stoppers, etc.

Smarten up new corks, or cork stoppers, quickly by melting a layer of coloured sealing wax over the top and pressing something decorative into the hot wax—a butter mould perhaps. The wax will also help keep the corks in place, and make the container airtight.

Fold a length of ribbon round the neck of the bottle or jar as well, and stick that down with another blob of sealing wax.

Screw-Tops, Lids, Tins, etc.

Brighten these all up at once by spreading them out on sheets of newspaper and spraying with gold, or coloured paint. Tins must first be stripped of paper labels and rubbed all over with wire wool to encourage the paint to stick. Spray twice over for best results. Paste on decorated labels, Christmas stickers, etc.

The Hamper Itself

One says 'gift hamper' without necessarily meaning a basket—most of us would use a cardboard box. (If you do have an old picnic basket kicking about, mind you, it is still a light, strong and very attractive way to pack this sort of gift.) Do take extra care when packing the jars and bottles: it would be tragic if they arrived broken after you had gone to so much trouble. Use a big box with room to spare. If you have any commercial packing materials available—pads, rigid containers, polystyrene—make use of them. Straw looks clean and attractive as a packing material for food, otherwise use crumpled newspaper, and lots of it. Seal up the box everywhere with gummed brown strip paper, then tie round with plastic string and get the post office to stick 'Fragile' labels all over the outside.

Pot Pourri

It's roses, roses all the way—or nearly, for pot pourri. Choose a dry day, and pick about 36 roses after the dew has dried on them. Spread the petals on paper and leave to dry indoors in a warm but airy place. Turn frequently and leave till almost as dry as paper. Pick and dry separately any other scented leaves and flowers you may have—lavender, rosemary, carnation, acacia, jasmine, orange blossom, scented geranium leaves, lemon scented verbena, bay leaves, eau de cologne, mint, etc. Use up to one handful of each. Add a sprinkling of bright, scentless petals to improve the look of the pot pourri—larkspur and marigold perhaps. Some people add some very thinly peeled lemon and orange rind.

Put dried rose petals into a pottery or glass container with a tight lid. Allow about 4 oz. salt for each handful of rose petals. Cover and leave for 5 days, stirring twice daily.

Meanwhile prepare a mixture of the following: 4 oz. powdered orris root, 1 oz. coriander seed, 1 oz. grated nutmeg, 1 oz. whole cloves, 2 to 3 sticks cinnamon, ½ oz. oil of lavender or geranium (optional). Allspice, mace and musk can be added, and you can vary the proportions to suit your nose.

At the end of 5 days mix the rose petals and salt with other dried flowers and leaves. If using oils, mix them with some of the orris root and other spices. Add the spices to the dried flowers, stirring all together and cover. Leave for 3–4 weeks, stirring occasionally. If it seems too moist add more orris, if too dry, more salt. Extra flowers and leaves can be added from time to time but they must be well dried first. Put into bowls, jars or sachets.

Lavender Bottles

Once upon a time almost every country-raised child learnt how to make lavender bottles, or faggots. A bunch of them would be hung in the linen cupboard to scent the linen, and young girls used them as markers between the sets of dozens and half-dozens in their dower chests. (Never let loose lavender flowers near anything made of wool as they cause tiny holes like moth bites.)

To make a lavender bottle pick 11 lavender flowers with long stalks, and make them up while the stalks are still pliant. The best time to pick the flowers is when the buds are just bursting. You will need 1–1½ yards of narrow (½ inch) baby ribbon. Lavender or yellow looks prettiest. Bunch the lavender heads closely together and tie ribbon tightly just underneath, leaving one short end of ribbon and one long one (see illustration).

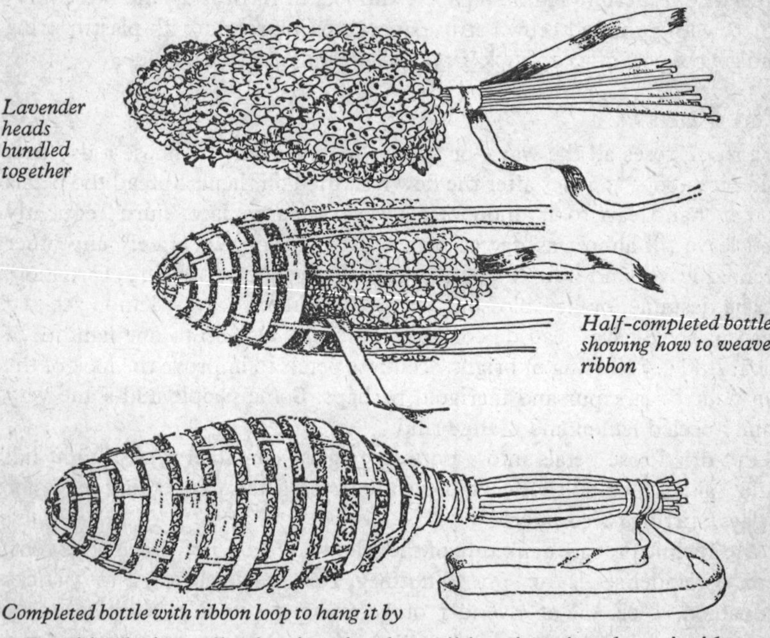

Lavender heads bundled together

Half-completed bottle showing how to weave ribbon

Completed bottle with ribbon loop to hang it by

Bend back the stalks, leaving the short ribbon hanging down inside, and weave the long end of ribbon in and out of the stalks till you have covered the last bit of the heads. Wind the long bit of ribbon round once or twice to make it fast and then tie a bow using the short end. Trim the stalks off evenly. For a more elegant finish allow ½ yard more ribbon, and carry the ribbon down to the end of the stalks, fastening again and leaving a ribbon loop to hang the bottle by.

Presents in Envelopes

Postage is so expensive these days and tying up parcels such a chore, I thought it might be helpful to include ideas for small presents, light and flat enough to be pushed into an envelope and dropped into the nearest letter box.

Set of Stencils

A set of ready-to-use stencils for decorating walls, furniture, lampshades, etc. would be an original present for the sort of people who are always trying out new ideas in their home. The size you cut them depends what use you have in mind for them—wall stencils can be 6 to 8 inches high, and wide in proportion, whereas stencils for decorating furniture would be about half that size. I have illustrated some stencil designs you could copy, borders as well as single motifs. They are all American, mostly 19th century. Designs like these are coming back into fashion, as people explore new ways of adding highly individual patterns and colours to their surroundings.

Materials

Stencil board (artists' suppliers, craft shops), sharp knife, sheet of glass for cutting on, pencil, rubber, carbon paper, large envelope.

To Make

Rough out the design on a sheet of paper before transferring it to the stencil board. Symmetry and precision does matter with stencils, so take care over this. Use compasses to draw circles, and make sure both halves of a motif are identical. The easiest way to do this is to draw one half of the motif out on fine tracing paper with Indian ink. Fold down the centre of the motif, so that the inked outline shows through the other half of the paper. Trace off, again using Indian ink. Then open out and the traced outline will show through clearly on the right side, completing the motif.

Use carbon paper to transfer the completed motif to your stencil board. When you have transferred the stencil pattern to the stencil board—allowing a good 2 or 3 inches of board all round the design—cut out this section with the Stanley knife and a ruler. The whole stencil can be any size, but I should let the size of the large envelope govern this. The design should be centred in the stencil, to make it easier to position accurately when it is used. Now lay the rectangle of board on your sheet of glass, and cut round the design with the point of the Stanley knife. Don't rush this as a clean cut is important, though you can tidy up jagged edges with a razor blade afterwards. Remove the cut-out areas. Tidy up rough edges. Write a line of explanation along the bottom—otherwise they may wonder what this see-through Christmas card is about.

Pretty Notebooks

Most stationers stock small plain paper notepads at a few pence each. Given really attractive covers, these make ideal small presents; they are quick and easy to make and you can post them off in envelopes. One sheet of patterned paper covers a stack of pads, so you can afford to get the nicest paper available. Alternatively, cover them in offcuts of hessian or felt (see Suppliers' Index).

Materials

Plain paper jotters, large sheet of mounting card (art shops), plain paper for linings, patterned paper or fabric for covers, Stanley knife, scissors, metal ruler or straight edge, glue size, Polycell.

Binding the jotter

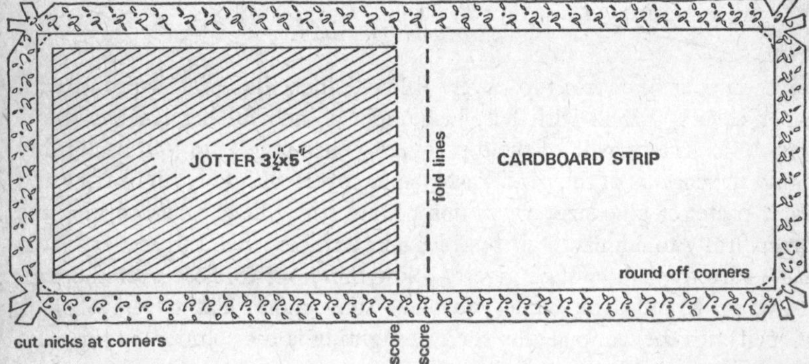

To Make

Polycell, or ordinary flour and water paste, is handy for sticking paper as it doesn't leave finger marks or smears. Glue size is best for sticking hessian as it glazes and stiffens the cloth as well as glueing it.

The notebook cover is made from a continuous strip of card, scored to fold over neatly at the top. It should be slightly larger than the jotter—about ¼ inch extra all round, and the spine should be fractionally wider than the top of the pad. Measure the first cover carefully and use it as a model for the rest. To cut the card, neatly lay a metal ruler or straight edge along the pencilled cutting line and draw the Stanley knife blade firmly along, pressing hard. With practice you should be able to cut through cleanly in one stroke. Round off the corners as shown and score lightly along the fold lines on both sides of the card, taking care not to cut right through. If you make a mistake you can stick the edges together again with a piece of gummed strip both sides. Any ragged edges and corners can be smoothed by rubbing with fine sandpaper. Use the card cover as a pattern

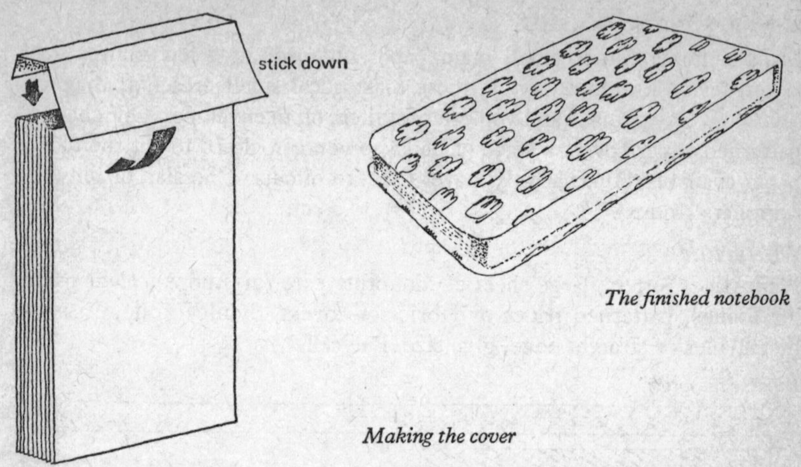

The finished notebook

Making the cover

for the paper or fabric top cover. Allow $\frac{1}{2}$ inch foldback all round with paper covers, $\frac{3}{4}$ inch with felt, just under 1 inch for hessian because it frays. Nick the corners of the top cover to encourage it to fold back tidily round the corners of the card. Paste paper covers with Polycell or flour and water paste (or glue size, if you don't mind sticky fingers), smoothing the paper firmly to eliminate air bubbles and wrinkles. Bend the cover too, to make sure there is enough give to allow the cover to close over the pad. Leave to dry off a bit while you make some more. The cover will look warped with the damp at this stage: weighting is the solution to this, and greatly improves the look of the pads. When you have completed a stack of covers, wrap a piece of plastic (I use old plastic bags cut up into squares) round each notepad. Slip the pad into the cover. Stand the pads in their covers in a pile, and lay several heavy books on top. Leave overnight. The plastic sheets prevent the jotters sticking to the covers. Next day, cut plain paper linings for all the covers, paste these in place, and paste a slip of paper over the top of the jotter as shown, sticking the free end to the back of the cover. Insert plastic sheets between pad and front cover, and weight as before. You can dispense with the plastic sheets if you have been neat with the paste and there is no likelihood of it oozing out and gumming your pad and cover together.

Note. When sticking hessian with size, saturate the hessian and brush size over the card too. Size doesn't give impact adhesion with fabrics, so you may have to wrap plastic round the cover to hold it in place while it dries. If this sounds like too much trouble, switch to Copydex, but I find size gives such a good finish, once dry, that I prefer to use it despite this disadvantage.

Hand-Decorated Labels for Food Containers

Imaginative cooks would appreciate a set of hand-decorated labels to paste onto the heterogenous collection of containers they keep their herbs, spices and other ingredients in. You will really score if you keep pace with their more exotic tastes and fads. In the herb line, include basil, chervil, oregano, dill, and French tarragon, as well as the standard thyme, marjoram and rosemary. Indian food fanciers who grind their own spice mixtures will want labels for cardamom pods, cumin, turmeric, fenugreek, coriander, black and white poppy seeds, dried red chillis. Wholefood eaters could probably do with identification tags for their millet, soy beans, sesame paste, wheat germ, miso, long and round brown rice, to name but a few; while Chinese food buffs need identification for such exotica as lily buds, star anise, sesame oil, rice vinegar, oyster sauce, mung beans, cloud ear mushrooms.

Ideas for decorated labels

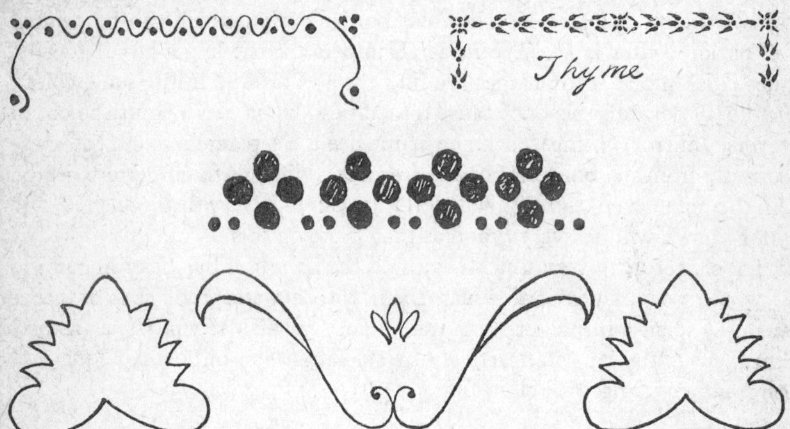

To Make

Self-adhesive labels are the handiest for the recipient though the paper is usually inferior and doesn't show off your art work to best advantage. Small packs of self-adhesive labels as sold for jam in most stationers, could double for herbs and spices. Larger plain white gummed labels, if you can get hold of them, need their corners rounding off as they tend to peel off otherwise. Or cut them to a nice oval shape. Most distinguished of all are labels cut from a good quality fine white drawing paper. This relies on your recipients having a pot of paste handy, but with such elegant labels who could grudge that effort? Cut a cardboard model and draw round it to ensure that the labels are all the same size. Cut out with sharp scissors.

To Decorate

The decoration can be as restrained or elaborate as time and talent allow. Using coloured felt pens, draw in decorative borders round the labels—different coloured stripes, dots and squiggles, tiny leaves (see illustrations). Print the name in the middle in your clearest hand (pencil first to try the effect) with Indian ink, or write it in sloping copperplate, using a calligrapher's pen or old fashioned nib pen. Sepia or brown ink looks pretty for writing copperplate. You can cheat by using Letraset small print for the names, though this could work out somewhat expensive if you do a lot of labels. A sprayed gold border looks handsome: make a smaller card panel to fit inside your labels and mask off the plain section while you spray the border. The size of this depends on the depth of border you want. Then place label face up on a large sheet of newspaper, clamp the card panel on top and spray, following maker's instructions. Repeat with each label. Most striking of all, make a lino-cut border design which can be printed off on label after label. (See under Hampers for the know-how.) Ideally, these look nicest if the names are lino cut and printed in the same colour as the border, but this does cause difficulties—the lettering must be cut in reverse (mirror writing), each new name needs a separate lino cut (do these separate from the border of course), and it is difficult to cut letters neatly. All the same, even slightly crude lettering can look very distinguished, and your friends will feel very grand as they paste on this unique set.

Labels get dirty very quickly with all the handling by sticky fingers, so it would be thoughtful to finish them with a waterproof coat of paper varnish, spirit varnish, or matt watercolour varnish if you prefer a matt finish. Pack the labels attractively by stacking them on a small square of card and covering with cling-film.

Notelets

Prettily decorated writing paper with matching envelopes is a sure-fire gift for girls in the nine to fourteen age group. Instead of buying the made-up packs, which are expensive, make your own sets of notelets and envelopes. A good way of remembering yourself to all those god-daughters, long lost nieces, etc. Buy a supply of small writing pads and matching envelopes in pretty colours. Sort these out into sets. The commercial packs supply twelve sheets of paper and six envelopes as a rule, but you could afford to be more generous, at least with the paper. Now for the decoration, which is vital. The quick, cheating solution is to buy sets of transfers and print these off in the top right-hand corner of each sheet. (The range of transfers is somewhat limited to date, although there are plans to bring out a series based on Victorian scraps in the near future.) More enterprising—and much cheaper—work out your own designs, copying shamelessly from such sources as wild flower guides (dainty wild roses, poppies, etc. are always popular), bird books and horse manuals. Trace or copy in pencil, Indian ink round and paint in delicately with watercolours, acrylics, or poster paints using fine brushes. This is a performance at first, but it is surprising how quickly one can produce a small design with a little practice. A lick of paper or spirit varnish over the design will make it look twice as professional. Arrange packs attractively on a sheet of card and cover with cling-film.

Note. Sober paper and no-nonsense transfers or pictures (or Disney again) would make this an acceptable present for a lad.

Paper Dolls

I suspect anyone with a feeling for clothes and colour would have as much fun designing and painting a paper doll and her wardrobe as a small girl would have playing with one. A nice gift for a younger sister, perhaps.

Choose the type of doll that you think would appeal to the child concerned—a chubby child doll is one possibility, or a 'pretty lady'. The clothes must follow suit of course, ultra grand for the pretty lady, demure for little chubby-cheeks. Invent your own paper doll, or copy one from a book or magazine—there is no shortage of models around. As children's standards of beauty don't vary much, give whichever doll you choose golden hair, long eyelashes, large bright eyes, rosy cheeks. Use white or cream mounting board for the doll herself. Draw her in pencil first, then Indian ink. Paint in the usual watercolours, gouache (particularly effective for this sort of work), acrylics or poster colours. Cut round her with a sharp Stanley knife blade, keeping the general outline simplified—too many indentations will weaken the doll. (Incidentally, it is as well to give her a restrained hairstyle so that clothes tags can be fitted over her shoulders.) Varnish over the doll with spirit or paper varnish, or matt watercolour varnish, to protect the surface. When dry, lay under heavy books to press flat. You can glue a tag to her back so that she will stand up.

Using the doll as a model, draw her a complete wardrobe on drawing book paper which will take paint without puckering up badly. Include hats, bags, boots, evening dress, as well as the more usual garments. Ink round them all with Indian ink including the tags, but don't cut them out unless the child is too young to use scissors. Paint them—or perhaps paint just a few, leaving her to do the rest—as above. Press flat under books. Pack doll and sheets of paper with clothes as for other paper items above.

Sew Cards

A cheap, easy-to-make present for both girls and boys in the four to seven age group (I used to love laboriously dragging my blunt needle in and out of these as a child and watching the shape materialise).

To Make

Cut light cardboard (shirt boards are good) into equal-sized cards about 5 by 6 inches. Work out some simple outlines of familiar animals: elephant, cat, mouse, duck, etc. (any child's picture book will help here), and convert these into dots spaced about $\frac{3}{4}$ inch apart. Print off the dotted lines onto your cards through carbon paper and punch a hole through each dot, using a darner or sharp knitting needle. Give the child encouragement—and a clue to the identity of the animal—by adding some painted details such as whiskers, eyes and bows. I would not bother to give the holes numbers as small children ignore these as a rule. Complete the set with several skeins of bright wool and a blunt tapestry needle stuck down to the top card with a bit of sellotape. Wrap in cling-film.

Make a Super Present out of a Simple Toy

Some small toys which might seem a bit niggardly on their own can be transformed by providing them with an imaginative context. One of those tiny plastic dolls with eyes that open and shut would make a charming present for a little girl if it arrived dressed and in a raffia Moses' basket. A set of doll's clothes, made from scraps, or bought, is twice as appealing packed into a little case inscribed with the favourite doll's initials. A set of plastic animals, in pairs, cries out for a traditional Noah's Ark as a habitat.

Moses' Basket

To make a doll-sized Moses' basket you need 1 yard of ¼-inch piping cord and a hank of natural raffia (craft shops, some gardening centres and pet shops). Thread a blunt tapestry needle with a long strip of raffia. Wrap the first inch or so of the piping cord with raffia and coil, stitching as you go, one stitch simply wrapping round the cord, the next going over two cords at once. Carry on like this, shaping the work into an oval rather than round shape till you have a base long enough to take the doll comfortably. Then begin curving the stitched cord up and out in the classic Moses' basket shape. When the basket is deep enough to accommodate the doll plus shawl and pillow, finish off by fraying out the end of the cord and binding down tightly with raffia. Make handles by buttonholing with raffia over raffia loops either side of the basket. Make a tiny pillow with cotton stuffed with cottonwool, and knit a coloured square to use as a blanket, or bind a square of fine wool with ribbon. Dress the doll simply in a white nightgown tied round the waist with tape, and a nappy held with tiny safety pins.

Doll's Suitcase

Woolworth's sell small cardboard cases with handles which are ideal for a doll's trunk. They look more distinguished if you paint them a shiny, cheerful colour outside and line the inside with patterned paper or printed cotton. Use glue size for sticking down fabric linings, and tuck raw edges under before glueing. Paint initials on with enamel paint using a fine sable brush. As a finishing touch you can make a small identification label for the handle by sandwiching a piece of white card, printed with the appropriate name and address, between two pieces of clear plastic and binding round with black adhesive tape. Tie on with a piece of string.

I am not giving patterns for dolls' clothes for the simple reason that dolls don't conform to a standard size, not yet, at least, but you might find the following suggestions helpful. For the under-fives keep the clothes simple, and easy to pull on and take off. Small knitted garments made from oddments of wool are probably best. A knitted cap with pompom, pullover and knitted tights kept up by elastic would be excellent. Otherwise go for loose garments with as few seams as possible. I find small children faced with an intractable doll's arm and a small armhole usually end up pulling off the arm and tearing the dress. A pair of long lace-edged drawers, plus a long loose smock of a dress and a simple long coat (make it from felt) to go over the top would strike most small girls as a glamorous outfit. Use press studs for fastenings. Do not spend time on 'dressmaker' details because these are wasted on small children. Instead, provide a shiny ribbon sash for the dress, and embroider a few lazy daisy flowers round the neck of the felt coat.

Older girls—five to ten—would appreciate the charm of little buttons, tucking, leather shoes, etc. So if this sort of miniature dressmaking appeals to you, you can really go to town. Provide a complete change of clothes—night clothes and day clothes for instance—so the child can enjoy dressing and undressing the doll. Make shoes from old leather gloves. Little strips of fur round the collar and cuffs of a coat, a quilted cotton dressing gown, lace trimmed underclothes, are all grown-up details which would appeal to a small girl.

Noah's Ark

One of the better contributions plastic has made to the quality of life, so far as I am concerned, is plastic animals. They are neatly and nicely made, they look right, and they are blessedly tough. The ideal habitat for a plastic menagerie (chosen in pairs of course) is a traditional, brightly painted Noah's ark like the ones produced to keep Victorian children quiet on the Sabbath—because of the biblical associations, an ark was considered to be an improving toy. Improving or not, an ark plus half a dozen pairs of plastic animals (you can go on adding to these on subsequent birthdays and Christmasses) is a plaything which keeps young children happily absorbed for hours on end. Popular with parents too, as it solves the perennial problem of where to stow all the darling little pigs and lions and moo-cows. My husband made the toy ark shown here in an afternoon. Its outward appearance is closely modelled on a Victorian museum piece, but he made free use of modern aids like thixotropic adhesive for assembling the various parts. The whole construction is held together by Thixofix—no screws or nails—and so far has proved remarkably sturdy. The ark was made of standard deal and plywood. Painting it up took a couple more sessions. I gave it two coats of undercoat, and thoroughly went over any cracks and dents in between, using a special plastic-based wood grain filler (see below). For the final colour scheme I used artists oil colours mixed into white undercoat. This is the best way to reproduce the colours on the Victorian toy, and if you buy the smallest size tubes of artists' oils it is also the cheapest. Two coats of polyurethane varnish to finish up with preserve and protect the paintwork as well as giving the toy the bandbox shiny look children find irresistible.

Note. Mr and Mrs Noah are not available in plastic. If you feel, as I do, that an ark slightly loses its point without this estimable pair in charge, you can model them very easily from Das and paint them up to look just like the traditional couple.

Materials

Ark: for the base you need a piece of 1-inch thick deal 16 inches long by 6 inches wide; for the house part, a piece of ⅛-inch plywood measuring 18 inches by 20 inches. You also need a 40-inch length of triangular wood section (we used lengths of old wooden stair rods) to make the internal scaffolding of the plywood house. Your wood merchant can probably supply offcuts of all these.

In the way of tools and other materials you will need a panel saw or power-operated jig saw, Surform plane (ironmongers), flat and rounded wood chisels, Dunlop Thixofix adhesive (ironmongers), 1 small tin white undercoat, 1 tube Japlac Spachtel wood filler (paint shops), small tubes of the following artists' oils (art shops)—yellow ochre, Venetian red, cobalt, burnt umber. 1 bottle Indian ink, 1 small tin polyurethane varnish in clear or natural. Also brushes—1 standard ½-inch paintbrush, plus 1 sable brush for fine detail. Lastly, masking tape, medium sandpaper, white spirit.

To Make

The ark: begin with the keel. Saw out the shape from the 1-inch deal. Use the Surform plane—a simplified plane which operates on wood like a grater on a carrot—to round off the sides and undercut the prow and stern to suggest a boat. Now mark off the position of the ark on top of the keel—

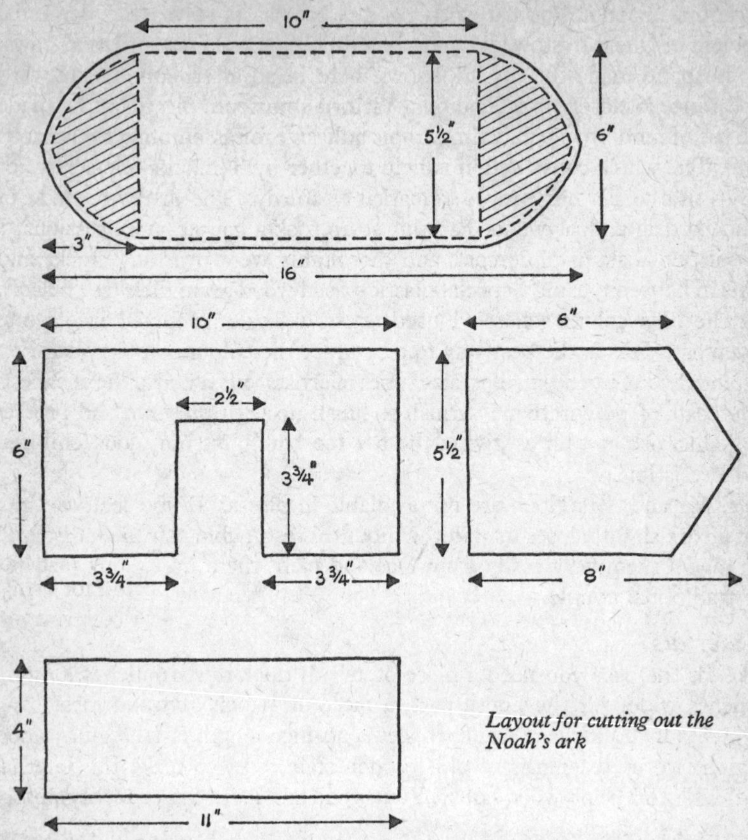

Layout for cutting out the Noah's ark

it should come squarely in the middle. In order to help along the illusion of a boat, you will need to do a little wood carving at this point, hollowing out the shaded areas in the diagram on either side of the ark to make it look more realistic. Mark round the shaded areas with a pencil. Then with the flat wood chisel incise round pencilled lines to a depth of approximately ¼ inch, tapping firmly but gently on your chisel with a hammer. The idea of this is to confine the hollowing-out operation within the incised lines and prevent you chipping off a chunk of prow as you gouge out the wood. Deal is soft but brittle, so chips may come off however careful you are. Don't worry about this—simply stick them back into place with Thixofix, following maker's instructions. Your scooped-out areas need not be perfectly smooth and flat, a few chisel grooves look suitably hand-finished.

Smooth off the keel with sandpaper.

Now for the ark itself—i.e. the house part. Measure and pencil the walls and two roof sections on plywood. Note that you will only cut one door, in the middle of one of the ark's longer walls. Cut round the outlines. Sand all edges smooth. Fit four walls together and sellotape to keep them in position while you cut lengths of triangular section to fit neatly into the four corners. These are glued into place in the corners to hold the little house together. Coat right-angled sides of these short lengths and inside corners of the ark walls with Thixofix and glue into place following maker's instructions carefully. When dry and solid, stand ark in place on keel, and cut two smaller lengths of section to fit at either end of the ark between the wall and keel. Coat these short pieces and the areas of wall which they will be fastened to and keel as before. Coat right round the base of the ark too, and run a little more Thixofix round the pencilled outline on the keel. Stick all together. Thixofix is a contact adhesive, but it's a good idea to loop some string round ark and keel to hold them together while the adhesive sets hard. If, like me, you tend to be sceptical about wonder-adhesives, you will be astonished at the strength and solidity of the final result—our ark has been played with for months, and is as solid as ever, which is more than one can say for a lot of toys. There is a reason for using adhesive rather than nails, screws, etc., which is that plywood is very difficult to drive nails into without splitting.

Painting and Finishing the Ark

Lightly sand all surfaces. Then coat the whole toy, inside the ark, under the keel and all—not forgetting the two roof sections—with undercoat. When dry, use the Spachtel filler to level up the grain of the plywood ark and roof sections, following maker's instructions. This doesn't take long and makes for a nice, smooth paint surface. Sand lightly all over. Then give the toy another coat of undercoat as before. When it is dry, you can paint in the original colours. I copied the original scheme because it was particularly pretty and decorative, but you might prefer to work out your own scheme, using quite different colours—red, white and blue was a patriotic combination the Victorians often used. Experiment with different colours on a sketch to try the effect—use watercolours or crayons.

The Victorian ark had pale blue walls decorated with painted windows and narrow bands of pink and yellow, a warm red brown roof relieved by cream scallopping to suggest tiles, and a darker brown keel. Some wall areas were left white for contrast. With a ruler, lightly pencil the areas to be painted blue and those to be striped pink and yellow. Mask off any areas to be left white with masking tape.

To mix up the pale blue wall colour, tip a little white undercoat into an old saucer. In another container dissolve a small blob of cobalt and a touch of yellow ochre in a little white spirit. Stir this into the undercoat a little at a time till you get a pretty duck-egg blue. Coat all pale blue wall areas with this, brushing on carefully and evenly. You will be able to paint roof sections and keel in the same session. Mix up roof colour like this. Dissolve burnt umber and Venetian red in a little white spirit to make a warm red brown, then mix this into a very little white undercoat. Paint roof sections with this. For the keel mix burnt umber with a spot of Venetian red into a very little undercoat as before (the undercoat merely gives colours grip, consistency and drying speed) and paint as much of the keel as possible without smudging—you can prop the toy on an improvised platform to get at the underneath. When dry, you may find the coloured areas need a second coat. Mix up colours as before and give them a second coat. It doesn't matter if your second coats are slightly different in tone, a little irregularity adds to the charm of hand-made toys. When dry, you are ready to paint in the decorative details, which is great fun. Using chalk or charcoal (easier to rub out than pencil) draw window outlines and a narrow frame round the door. Using 10p coins, draw little circles on the eaves. Mix Venetian red into a very little white undercoat, and using the sable brush (you can use masking tape for perfect accuracy, but I don't think this is vital), outline the windows, circles and door frame in red, then fill in with a wider brush. When dry, use sable brush and Indian ink to paint in little black window panes and black daisy motif on circles. Paint narrow black lines round door frame. Mix a very little Venetian red into white undercoat to give a pale pink. Use this to paint in the pink band as shown. When dry, peel off top masking tape. Stick tape down both sides of the yellow band. Mix yellow ochre into white to give a warm yellow and paint in yellow band. Add more white undercoat to give cream, and with sable brush, brush in scallopped tile patterns along both roof sections. When dry, varnish the whole toy. Sand this very lightly when dry, and re-varnish. Cut a strip of leather—preferably brown or black—long enough to make a hinge for roof sections and glue this down (use Evostik) along the roof ridge. More leather hinges stuck down crosswise inside will strengthen the roof. Optional: you can make a small gangplank from a scrap of ply for animals to enter the ark by. Paint this roof colour. I left the inside of the ark white, except the floor.

Mr and Mrs Noah

With Das, model figures keeping them to scale with ark and animals—i.e. smaller than a giraffe but big enough to keep lions in order. Insert wire crooks into the models while Das is still pliable. When completely dry, touch up any cracks with more Das or Polyfilla. Leave to dry again. Varnish all over. When dry, paint with oil colours in undercoat as for the ark. When quite dry, paint in detail with Indian ink. Varnish.

Noah's ark with Mr and Mrs Noah

Presents for the Home

Folk Art in Fire Cement

Fire cement, in case you have not come across it, is sold in tins for filling in gaps round solid fuel heaters, chimneys, etc. It handles as easily as clay or plasticine, and can be baked in an ordinary domestic oven till it is hard and as weighty as stone. And as things go these days, it's cheap. It lends itself very happily to modelling colourfully painted ornaments like the goat and cat illustrated, both of which were inspired by early American chalk sculpture. If the idea of making figures as presents appeals to you, I suggest you interpret folk designs too, at least to begin with, as the shapes are simple enough for amateurs to model and the painted finish makes them gay and charming to have around in almost any setting. For other examples to copy look through shops stocking Mexican, Peruvian and Indian wares, coffee table books on folk art, primitive cultures, etc. (visit your local library). I will give the drill for making up one of the figures in some detail, as this can be adapted for others.

Folk art goat and cat made of fire cement

Painted Goat

This was modelled round a wire skeleton, which sounds more of a business than it is. It only takes a minute or two to bend and twist wire into a crude frame to build your figure around. In the case of the goat some sort of support was essential to prevent the horns sagging and the legs buckling while the cement was soft. Compact, all-of-a-piece shapes like the cat illustrated, can be modelled without a skeleton, though you will probably find it is quicker in the end to make a frame than to keep straightening up your figure as you work on it.

Materials

One tin fire cement (the more you buy, the cheaper it is), pliers, stout wire (coat hanger), undercoat, acrylic colours, varnish, stone file.

To Make

With pliers cut and bend wire into a rough goat skeleton. The original figure was 8 inches high, ours is about 5. The size is up to you, but don't make it too small or the chunky charm will be lost. Take up a good-sized lump of cement and pat into a thickish oblong for the base. Stand wire shape on top and begin patting cement up all round the skeleton, starting with the legs. Keep the modelling basic at this stage, concentrate on getting a solid core for the figure. Details like tail, beard and subtle contours can be added after the first baking, so keep the first model under-weight, not over—remember you can add more on but you can't take it off once it has baked hard. Stick any heatproof props that come to hand under the goat's belly and chin to support these if they show a tendency to sag a little. Stand the figure on a baking tin and place in a low to moderate oven till baked quite hard and dry. Tap with a metal spoon to tell whether it's quite cooked—it should clink like brick or stone; if it makes a dull sound it's not quite cooked through. When cool, give the goat a careful going over, adding a tail, smoothing out his horns, fattening up his sides and generally rounding him out. Smooth the cement surface by sleeking it with wet fingertips. Bake again.

Before painting it's a good idea to refine the surface with a stone file, though this is not essential. Too rough and grainy a surface detracts from the painted finish, I feel, but don't go for satin smoothness either. Give the goat one thick coat of white undercoat. Dry thoroughly. We copied the original paintwork: first the goat had a watery wash of vermilion brushed lightly over the undercoat to tone down the whiter-than-whiteness. This wash should be *very* thin to produce the merest blush of colour. Next the spots, stripes, features, beard and tail were painted in using a thinner dilution of acrylic for the spots, thicker for more emphatic details like beard and tail. The base was painted ochre yellow. Don't fuss too much over getting everything just so—each stripe parallel and the same thickness —these folk figures were dashed off at top speed, and a spontaneous, irregular look is half the secret of their charm. When dry, varnish the figure once or twice to protect the paint and to give it a bright and shiny look. If the shine seems too pronounced, rub down the varnish gently with soft wire wool.

The original cat colours are dull ochre yellow overall, with black spots, leg stripes, eyebrows, claws and whiskers, red outlines round ears, red neck ribbon, tawny yellow eyes with black pupils and white whites.

Note. Unpainted, fire cement dries to a quite pleasing pale stone grey, suitable for making replicas of small stone carvings, gargoyles, etc.

Drawn Thread Table Mats

Drawn thread work is traditionally associated with Irish linen, which looks elegant but is a chore to wash and starch. To my mind it looks even more effective worked on hessian, which comes in 6-foot widths, a superb range of colours, and costs around a pound a yard. Contrary to what the suppliers tell you, hessian washes very well, though you must allow for shrinkage, which means a hot water wash before you cut out the mats. The original dressing will be washed away, but pressing with a hot iron over a damp cloth brings up the finish handsomely again. Drawn thread work is a cinch to do, even if you have never tackled embroidery before, and progresses very quickly. A set of four or six hessian mats would be a smashing present for friends who do a lot of entertaining. The darker, offbeat colours—brown, cinnamon, olive, coffee—look good with modern pottery or china and stripped pine. Or, for a seasonal touch, why not do a set in a bright, brave scarlet—good with plain white china.

To Make

You need 1 yard of hessian for six mats, and matching thread. Before washing the hessian run a line of machining round the raw edges to check fraying. Press the material when dry. The size of the mats depends to some extent on the size of the table they will go on. I find 20×15 inches a good generous size, which allows room for cutlery and glasses as well as a large dinner plate. If your friends have a narrow table, reduce both measurements by 1 inch. To make sure you cut all the mats on the exact straight of the hessian, mark off the mats—three across the width, two along the length—and draw threads at each point. Cut the mats out. Again run a line of machining round the edges to check fraying. The measurements allow for ¾–1 inch all round for hems. Mark off a point 2¾ inches in from each corner of the mat on both sides, and at each point draw out three threads. Now, with a needle threaded with matching cotton or a matt-textured synthetic thread, stitch down either side of this group of drawn threads from the back. The idea is to catch down the threads, two or three at a time, leaving regular spaces between the bundles. The stitches which catch the threads down to the body of the mat should be small, otherwise they will show up on the right side of the finished mat. You can suit yourself whether you pick up two or three threads with each stitch: two gives smaller spaces, three quite pronounced squares when both sides are stitched. Repeat for each drawn thread panel. Turn back the hems and hand-stitch or machine them down all round. Press the mat carefully.

Pretty Boxes

Light bentwood boxes, which can be bought very cheaply in their unfinished state, can be transformed with paint and varnish into highly decorative objects. Give them away as they are (no one ever has too many little boxes); fill them with home-made sweets or salted nuts (see Arabella Boxer's *Christmas Food and Drink*) for an imaginative touch; or more practically, stuff them with the sort of cheap and useful item households are forever running short of—paper clips, rubber bands, safety pins, shirt buttons.

Don't imagine that you need overflowing artistic talent to paint a pretty box. Most of the decorative techniques described here are so simple a child could do them. Painted line trims are easy with masking tape. If you want to 'personalise' a box, you can add elegant initials in a minute with Letraset transfer sheets.

A superfine finish is not obligatory, of course, and you can spend as little time as you wish over the priming, sanding and varnishing. However, it does make the boxes much nicer to handle and use, as well as strengthening the brittle wood, and gives your paintwork a sleek professional finish.

Note. The various finishes described could be applied just as well to odd boxes picked up at jumble sales, Oxfam shops or street markets. Glue back any loose bits, strip off lumpy paintwork with Polystrippa, or sand down till smooth, then coat with primer (wood primer for wood, metal for metal) and/or undercoat, and decorate in any of the styles suggested below.

Materials

Bentwood boxes (they come in various shapes and sizes, prices vary according to size), Araldite, primer or undercoat, poster paints or acrylic paints in a fair range of colours, assorted brushes, including sable ones, sandpaper, masking tape, Letraset transfer type, gold spray paint, varnish.

Preparing the Boxes

Sand them lightly all over, inside and out, to smooth off splintery patches and to even up the grain. Sand round the rims too, as these tend to be rough. Any cracks in the wood can be mended very efficiently with Araldite. Mix up a little Araldite on a scrap of glass or paper, coat the crack lightly on both sides, then bind the edges tightly together with strips of sellotape. Run a strip of sellotape along the crack, and you will find the adhesive dries to a perfectly flat, invisible mend. Unless you are using a folk style of decoration which looks attractive with the wood grain showing through, it is best to prime the wood before painting. This levels up the grain, strengthens the paintwork and brings up the paint colours. Use wood primer or white undercoat, or both. Coat the boxes thinly but thoroughly, inside and out, and leave to dry. Sand again, lightly, with fine sandpaper. They are now ready to decorate.

Spongeing

Spongeing was very popular with 19th-century folk painters who used it for anything from grandfather clocks to knife boxes. It is dazzlingly simple and quick to do. Depending on which colours you use, and how you wield your sponge, you can obtain effects ranging from a simple paw print to an intricate marbled or tortoiseshell effect. First decide on your colour scheme. (Don't be too rigid about this, because you can get marvellous effects accidentally, so allow for the unexpected.) Paw print decoration looks most effective in boldly contrasting colours—black on red, or vice versa, dark green on pale lemon yellow (add red line trims), gold on red. You can paint the inside of the box in the same colour scheme reversed, or just spray it gold.

First give the box, inside and out, two coats of whatever ground colour you have settled on. Poster and acrylic colours dry fast so the first box will be dry by the time you have finished painting. To sponge, dab some of the colour full strength on a saucer, dip in a scrap of sponge (real sponge is best) and dab over the surface. Check the print first on a piece of paper to judge the effect. You may need to water down the paint a little, as a thick, impasto effect will leave the box surface lumpy. To obtain bold prints bunch up the sponge. Space the prints out, too, so that it looks as if the box had been delicately walked over. When the paw printing is dry, you can add line trim in a contrasting colour round the rim. Stick on a strip of masking tape, leaving exposed the depth of rim that you want to paint, then paint over with red, or green or whatever colour you fancy. Or spray with gold paint, making sure that all the printed parts of the box are covered—use a piece of newspaper held in place with pins. When dry, peel off the tape. For a line trim set in from the edge, use two strips of masking tape set $\frac{1}{8}$ inch apart. Line trims round the top of the box are more difficult to do with tape, as it doesn't curve readily, so it is best to do these freehand with a fine sable brush over a chalked guideline. Or you can use felt pens if the colours are right. For black 'lining', use sable pencil and Indian ink.

Finish the box inside and out with one, or better, two, coats of varnish. It is worth varnishing the inside too as the lid will glide into place much more smoothly.

For a tortoiseshell look, the principle is the same, except that you superimpose spongeing prints in three colours—burnt sienna (any reddish brown paint would do), burnt umber and black, on a yellow ground coat. Sponge the burnt sienna first, using a slightly diluted colour, and aiming for a blurred overall print with some yellow showing through. Sponge the burnt umber next, concentrating the prints more, then sharpen up the mottled tawny effect with light, crisp, black prints here and there. Don't overdo the black. Gold line trim and gold inside look very handsome with this colour scheme. Use spray paint, as above, masking off the sides of the box when you spray inside the box and lid. Varnish.

Marbled effects are achieved in the same way as tortoiseshell, except that you use different colours and rather more water with them for a blurred watercolour look. Don't have the paint too watery, though, and do let one colour dry before you add the next, or you will end up with a streaky mess. The possible colour permutations are endless. Some I have found effective are: khaki green over cerulean blue, purple and brown over red, turkey red and denim blue over buff, salmon pink and sepia over stone grey. All these look prettier with contrasting line trim—use the darkest of the marbling colours for this. If you want to add initials, paint a small oval or circle on the lid in the palest colour you are using, or off-white. Alternatively, mask off this area while spongeing the box, then paint a fine line round the plain inset, and transfer the initials into the centre from the Letraset (see illustration). The print needs to be spot on to look good, one letter a fraction askew looks clumsy. Sketch the arrangement out first on paper and use chalk guidelines which can be rubbed off later. Varnish.

Stippled or Dragged Colours

This technique is similar to spongeing, but you use a brush not a sponge, and the pattern should be uniform. I find it looks particularly attractive done in lighter colours over a dark background—say green and yellow over brown, red and brown over black—as a subtly variegated background to a painted stencil (an owl stencil perhaps), or plain inset with initials as above. Stipple by dipping the tip of a coarse-bristled brush into concentrated colour and then jabbing lightly over the surface. A pale colour will appear to vanish into the darker base coat when dry, but don't be misled by this—varnishing will restore it to full strength. Dragging consists of brushing one colour over another using a coarse brush and dryish paint consistency, so

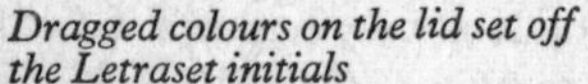

Dragged colours on the lid set off the Letraset initials

The finished box with a sponged decoration

that the base colour shows through the spaced brushmarks. These can be even for a finely striped effect, or broken up into swirls, zigzags or feathered effects. Finish with two coats of varnish.

Stencils

Stencils are the answer to decorating things at top speed. Cutting a stencil takes a few minutes, but after that you can brush the pattern on to your boxes in a flash. (See illustrations for suggested stencil patterns.) Stencil board can be obtained in large sheets from artists' supply shops. Or use brown paper varnished both sides to waterproof and stiffen it. You may want to invent your own stencil patterns, which is quite simple so long as you remember to break up the pattern in such a way that all the cut-out areas are linked up to the main body of the stencil by little 'ties'. Make a stencil by drawing the pattern on the paper or board, or transferring a careful drawing via carbon paper. Then lay the paper or board on a sheet of glass, and cut round with a sharp Stanley knife. Trim any ragged edges with a razor blade. To stencil, lay the stencil down on the surface to be patterned, hold down firmly with fingertips of one hand while you brush colour into the cut-out spaces with the other.

Tips to Remember

Cutting the stencil to the exact size and shape of your box lids—round or oval—helps you to position the design accurately and quickly each time. Use the paint colour thick, adding very little water, if any. Experiment on a piece of paper first. Mixing the colour with a special gel medium will prevent the colour running and smudging, but this is not essential. Professional stencillers used a brush like a shaving brush, or sash tool, with a jabbing or dabbing rather than brushing motion, but for small scale stencils almost any reasonably stiff brush—bristle, not camelhair or squirrel—will do the trick. The chief points to be careful about are not to move the stencil as you paint, and to lift it off quickly and deftly afterwards. Gold or coloured spray paint (cellulose paint for touching up car bodywork comes in an enormous range of colours and dries hard and shiny) can be used effectively with stencils for an untouched-by-hand look, if that is what you fancy. However, this is tricky to get just right, as the spray tends to be

Ideas for stencils

uneven, and, unless you hold the stencil down very firmly, some colour seeps underneath. But experiment on paper—you may have an inborn knack. Lacy plastic place mats make interesting ready-made stencils to use with spray paints, and you can use the mats afterwards for Christmas tree decorations. Sprayed gold both sides and hung from a red ribbon they look charming.

All Over Hand-Painted Motifs

Small, individually painted motifs—ladybirds, *fleurs de lys*, snowflakes, stars, strawberries—studded over a painted box, can look delightfully pretty. These are comparatively slow to do, but look expensive, and are a good way to cut your decorative teeth, as it were. Practise a single motif till you can reproduce it accurately, then put chalk spots on your box at regularly spaced intervals—after that it's just a matter of reproducing the

Suggestions for individual motifs

miniature design as carefully as you can. Make sure the base colour is uniform before painting the designs. White snowflakes on black, gold stars on red, gold *fleurs de lys* on a green base, are all good combinations. Paint the inside of the box a pretty contrasting colour and varnish.

Folk Decoration

Gaily coloured, simple folk designs are traditional decoration for this type of box, and are great fun to do once you have gained a little confidence in creating patterns and combining colours. Both the box lid designs illustrated are typical of the ones used by 19th-century folk painters; I have included them because they are particularly easy to copy. Decorative one-

Simple folk designs that are easy to reproduce

dimensional patterns like these can be tackled successfully by mere beginners. For more ideas take a look round the 'ethnic' shops—Indian painted clay toys and boxes, beautifully patterned eggs from Russia and Czechoslovakia, Mexican and Peruvian knick-knacks in brilliant sharp colours are all rich sources of perfected motifs and colour contrasts. Borrow and adapt as freely as you like, but sketch out any designs of your own first in colour to get an idea of the general effect. There cannot be any hard and fast rules about colour, but on the whole, bright clear colours painted on a dark background—green, blue, dark red—and relieved by plenty of white flicks or bands of painted 'featherstitch' is a reliable formula. You may want to try your hand at more ambitious, representational designs such as figures, animals or birds. In my experience it is difficult for a sophisticated adult to get these just right; the results tend to look self-conscious and fussy instead of spontaneous and fresh. One solution which can work very well is to coax a child (under seven) to draw a bird, pretty lady or whatever and reproduce the best of the results in your own colours.

Collage

Creating attractive, whimsical collage designs is something at which sophisticated adults excel, and they can look very chic decorating a small box. Cut out suitable shapes and scraps from magazines, old Christmas cards, postcard reproductions—the more varied in scale, style, etc., the better. Paint the box all over first in a suitable background colour. Use a good impact adhesive such as Bostik, Uhu or Evostick to stick on the scraps. It is more amusing—both to do and to receive—if the collage material relates in some way to the person for whom the box is destined. A choice collection of pin-ups for a Don Juan, bras and lighters for Women's Libbers, a spread of pop idols for impressionable teenagers. Make sure all the scraps are firmly stuck down—nothing looks sadder or more half-hearted than a peeling collage. Help the good work along by varnishing twice over, using a special spirit varnish which dries very quickly and gives paper a splendidly glossy finish. Rustin's clear spirit varnish (paint shops) is ideal for this.

Re-Finishing Whitewood

Many shops now stock whitewood kitchen ware which is excellent value. It comes in nice, simple shapes, and, being made of wood, is virtually indestructible—I'm particularly thinking of the eggcups. Anyone prepared to spend a little time and trouble putting an attractive, durable finish on a set of eggcups, or a spice rack, would have a very acceptable present for a modest outlay. The quickest way to achieve this is to sand the surface and apply one of the coloured varnish stains. Or you could turn the operation into a real labour of love, using wood filler, enamel paints and some simple hand-painted decoration.

Note. I would resist the temptation to jolly up wooden spoons in this way, because cooking utensils which come into contact with boiling fat and liquids should not be painted or varnished.

Materials

Medium and fine grade sandpaper, small tin of coloured varnish stain (available in a good range of strong bright colours) or wood filler, undercoat, coloured enamel paint, varnish.

Method I

This is the quickie method. First sand the eggcups or spice rack down very thoroughly, using the medium sandpaper. You will find a fair bit of sanding is needed to smooth off surface roughness and level up the wood grain. Try not to sand off all detail—fold the paper into a flat edge for working into angles. When the article feels reasonably pleasant to touch, move on to the fine grade sandpaper and carry on until it feels really smooth. If an odd bit snaps off with all this attention, don't worry—stick it back with Araldite and it will last as long as the thing itself. Now finish with the varnish stain, following maker's instructions. If you feel your eggcups look too plain as they are, you can add a simple painted border or paint on the names of all the members of the family. Use white or coloured enamel for this (the advantage being that you can buy these in very small tins) and fine brushes—sable or watercolour brushes. The enamel may need thinning with the special thinner sold by the makers, or cellulose thinners sold for use with car enamel. Professionals decorate objects-in-the-round—like eggcups—by setting them on a little revolving stand. You might be able to improvise one from an old portable gramophone turntable. It does mean you can decorate right round the thing without touching it and smudging the art work. Failing this, paint one section at a time. Leave to dry hard. You can varnish again, but enamels don't really require this.

Method II

Sand well with medium, then fine paper. You don't have to achieve such a fine finish, as you will be levelling off the grain with a filler: the cheapest for the purpose is Polyfilla. Use this after the first coat of undercoat. More expensively, there are plastic-based wood fillers sold in tubes, which do a very good job of sleeking a porous open-grained wood. These can be applied to the bare wood, saving one coat of undercoat. (A second coat of undercoat is advisable with Polyfilla, to bind it and prevent it flaking off.) Either way, apply the filler all over the object, inside and out, using a flexible spatula or knife, or your fingers. Leave to dry. Sand down with medium, then fine paper to level off the filler. Sand down any undercoats lightly, then finish with two coats of enamel paint, thinning the first to prevent too thick a paint build-up. Decorate with simple designs—a white dotted line makes an effective border—using enamel in a contrasting colour. For more elaborate decoration you might like to try the canal-boat painter's trick of mixing oil colours into ordinary undercoat. This is an easier paint to use than pure enamel for decorative painting, and mistakes can be wiped off easily with a rag and white spirit. Finish by varnishing, using a plastic-based varnish for strength—polyurethane or even floor seal.

Knife Rack

Any keen cook would welcome a knife rack to hang on the wall. This one is easy to make and the best for the knives as the magnets will not blunt a razor edge the way grooved holders do. Anyone with razor-edged cooking knives *should* get them up on the wall out of harm's way—rooting about in a kitchen drawer can lead to nasty cuts. A good present for a young lad to give his mum, I would think.

Materials

Length of ½ inch deal or pine approximately 1 foot by 3 inches, 6 pot and button magnets (ironmongers), Araldite, brass mirror plates, 4 small screws, sandpaper, varnish.

To Make

The length of the rack depends on the number of implements it is required to take—half a dozen would be a reasonable allocation for most cooks. When you have decided on the correct length and cut the plank accordingly, round off all the edges nicely with coarse, then fine sandpaper. Smooth the whole surface of the rack until it feels and looks pleasant. Varnish with polyurethane. When dry, rub down lightly with fine paper to get a super-smooth finish. Work out where you think the magnets should go—if the rack is to hold wide blades like cleavers as well as narrow ones like vegetable peelers, space the magnets accordingly, some wide apart, others bunched up. Keep them all smartly vertical, though. Coat the backs of the magnets very thinly with Araldite and lay in position on the rack. When they are all in place, lay a rigid board over the top and stand something heavy on top. Leave for 48 hours or so, till quite dry. Then screw the small mirror plates to the back of the rack, one at each corner. As a finishing touch you could print the word KNIVES across the top using Letraset, and finish with a dab of protective varnish.

Wall Letter Pocket

This letter pocket is a cardboard copy of a Victorian one made from papier-mâché. It looks pretty pinned to the wall beside a desk or writing table, and is handy for holding unanswered letters. It is a bit fiddly to make, but is an excellent present for a mother-in-law with a penchant for Regency stripes. I covered mine in a scrap piece of velveteen, trimmed with matching silk cord. You could substitute scarlet felt, which is nice to work with as it doesn't fray, or a prettily patterned paper.

Layout for the letter pocket *The finished article*

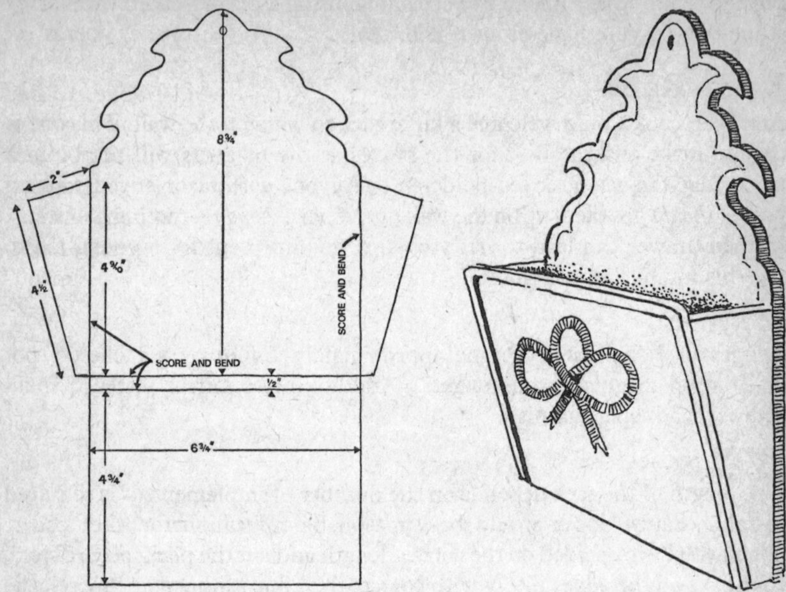

Materials

Sheet of rigid cardboard 14 × 10 inches, double that amount of fabric or paper for covering, gummed brown strip paper, adhesive (I used glue size, but Bostik or Polycell for fabric, or flour and water paste for paper would do equally well), sharp knife, scissors, cord or ribbon for trimming.

To Make

Make a pattern on brown paper, using the measurements shown in the accompanying diagram. The curlicue top may be a little difficult to reproduce accurately—draw it out in pencil till you think it looks right and cut round halfway. Fold over lengthwise and trace off round the cut edge to get the other side exactly matching. Fold the pattern along fold lines and check whether the side flaps match up with the front flap as shown in the diagram. Make any alterations necessary on the pattern. Now draw round the pattern on cardboard and lay the cardboard on the sheet of glass, or several sheets of newspaper. Cut round the outline with a Stanley knife. Using a ruler as a guide, score lightly back and front along dotted lines. Fold into knife edges. Cut the same shape twice over in cover fabric or paper, allowing ½ inch extra all round for turnback. One side of the letter holder is covered before making the side joins. This is the side that forms the back and inside front of the letter pocket. Coat one side of the cardboard cut-out and the back of the paper or fabric thinly and evenly with glue, paste or Bostik. Cut nicks at intervals along the curlicues on the back to allow the cover to be folded back neatly. Lay cover fabric or paper over card cut-out, centring them carefully. Smooth out cover to remove air bubbles and wrinkles, drawing it tight and smooth. Fold back turnback along the curlicues. Trim off extra fabric and paper round the rest of the cut-out, cutting it close to the card edge. Fold the letter holder up along bend lines for joining up. (Any creases in cover paper or fabric at the bottom of the pocket can be eased out now with a knitting needle or knife blade.) Stick gummed strip down over side joins to hold pocket together. Stick more gummed strip along all bend lines to strengthen them. Trim off neatly. Try outside cover over letter holder before pasting to see where it should be trimmed. Place back of letter holder on back cover section and draw round curlicues. Trim off. To prevent bulky overlaps of paper or fabric at side joins, trim off turnback at these points.

Coat cover section thinly with paste or glue and stick down over letter holder, smoothing it carefully over all the joins and drawing it as tight as possible. This outside cover piece, plus the gummed strip, will make the cardboard holder strong enough to stand up to daily use. Cord can be glued round all the outside edges as a decorative finish, or stitched in place if you have the time and the cover fabric is suitable. Alternatively, trim with ½-inch grosgrain ribbon, easing it round curves and corners. Use glue size for this job if possible, as it gives excellent adhesion when dry and leaves ribbon with a stiffly glazed finish which looks very professional. Finally, punch a hole at the top as shown to hang it up by. If the front of the letter holder looks too plain, add a frogged ornament of twisted cord, or a beaded or embroidered motif (haberdashery departments) glued or stitched in place.

Note. When using velveteen or a fraying fabric, this should be folded back and glued down. The back of the letter holder should be covered in matching felt, otherwise you will have an impossible task trying to get a neat finish round the curlicue top.

Bulletin Board

A felt covered bulletin board studded with brass-headed nails makes a handsome catch-all for the bits and pieces people like to hoard—newspaper cuttings, postcard reproductions, snaps, pop star pictures. A good present for almost anyone in the family. Choose a felt colour that goes with the décor.

Materials

Piece of chipboard measuring 24×18 inches, piece of felt 26×20 inches, roll of ½-inch cotton tape, brass-headed upholstery tacks, bayonet tacks,

Bulletin board

$7\frac{1}{2}$-foot length of $\frac{5}{8}$-inch beading for frame (optional), two brass mirror plates, Copydex or Evostik adhesive, tin of Dylon.

To Make

Dye the tape to match or contrast with the felt, following maker's instructions. Spread a thin coat of Copydex or Evostik over the chipboard and stick down the felt, starting at the middle and smoothing outwards. Draw the felt taut over the sides and stick down at the back. With chalk, mark off 6-inch intervals all the way round the board. Draw tapes across in a lattice pattern as shown, interlacing them where they cross and driving in bayonet tacks a little way to hold them in position temporarily. When all the tapes are in place, make any adjustments needed to get them taut and bang home the bayonet tacks. Hammer in brass-headed tacks at each tape intersection. Glue a piece of brown paper over the back and screw brass mirror plates into the top corners to hang the board by. You can neaten up the edges of the board by simply glueing tape all the way round. Or cut the beading to make a frame and knock this home all round with panel pins. It can be varnished, painted or simply sanded lightly and waxed.

Keyboard

A decoratively shaped and painted little wooden keyboard to take all the household keys is a useful, cheerful thing to hang up in the kitchen or near the front door. Make it from scraps of plywood, glued and clamped together to give enough thickness to take the screw hooks, or use an odd piece of chipboard or blockboard. Use a saw, or failing that a fretsaw to cut out the shapes.

To Make

Cut a paper pattern the size you want—6 – 8 inches high is about right for the heart and owl, 8 – 10 for the key. If you are using two thicknesses of ply, do the glueing and clamping first. Wipe the surfaces to be glued with a rag moistened with white spirit to remove any grease. Spread wood adhesive thinly over both surfaces, wait ten minutes, then clamp tightly with D-clamps (ironmongers, DIY shops) and leave to dry thoroughly. Trace round the pattern on to the wood with felt pen, and cut out with jig saw or fret saw. Sand the edges smooth with medium, then fine sandpaper. Paint the edges and both sides of the board with wood primer. Sand lightly, then paint with undercoat. Now give the board two top coats of whatever colour you fancy—for example, white for the owl, red for the heart, black for the key. Use tiny tins of Humbrol enamel or Japlac (paint shops). Sand very lightly between coats for a supersmooth finish. Now, with a fine brush and contrasting paint colour, add decorative details. Paint the key handle gold, perhaps; paint in the owl's features with red, and give him a brown twig to sit on; add white flicks and yellow and green flower shapes to the heart. When quite dry, varnish over the board, not forgetting the sides. Dry thoroughly. Now screw in brass hooks as shown, and screw a little mirror plate to the back to hang it by. A mirror plate is better than a screw eye for this, as a lot of keys can be surprisingly heavy.

Three wooden keyboards

SUPPLIERS' INDEX

Crafts Unlimited, 21 Macklin St, London WC1 is a useful address to know if you are planning a DIY Christmas. They run a mail order service and stock a wide variety of items mentioned in this book – cotton balls and shiny straw, light bentwood boxes, a comprehensive range of jewellery 'findings' – clasps, links, clips, chains etc. Also the special range of Deka paints for decorating glass and ceramics. Write for their price list. A bumper illustrated catalogue is available too, but you have to pay for that.

Dryad Handicrafts Ltd, Northgates, Leicester is another Mecca for hobbyists of all sorts. Their copiously illustrated catalogue (which you have to pay for) is an absorbing read. They also stock unpainted wooden items – candlesticks, boxes etc. – for decorating and anything you might need for home made jewellery. Also such elusive traditional materials as doctor's flannel (scarlet and cream), unbleached calico, muslin. If art shops in your area are unhelpful with such items as stencil board, gold leaf and size, lino printing equipment, all these can be obtained from Dryads, who run an efficient mail order service. The best time to order through the post is during the school holidays, before the rush begins.

The Felt and Hessian Shop, 34 Greville St, London WC1 stocks an immense range of felts and hessians in different weights, qualities and price ranges. The colour range is superb – samples of both supplied on request. One interesting service they offer, from the DIY point of view, is cheap offcuts of hessian or felt which are sold by the pound weight at prices well below the price by the yard. You have no choice of colours of course, but in my experience one gets good variety, including such Christmassy hues as red and green. They do a mail order service.

Donald MacDonald (*Antartex*) *Ltd*, Alexandria, Dumbarton, Scotland supply bags of lambskin squares (plain or curly) through the post for making up into jerkins, rugs or whatever. A bag of 70 squares (more than enough for a child's jerkin) costs £2.00 for the curly variety and £1.75 for the plain. The skins are excellent quality (the curly is particularly attractive) and they come in natural colours, cream or peat brown.

Barthes-Roberts Ltd, 59 Lant St, London SE1 is the best place to go for corks of every different size and shape. They are a wholesale firm, but they will supply to private individuals if you turn on the charm.

Gedge & Co., 88 St John St, Clerkenwell, London EC1, is a trade shop specialising in every kind of out-of-the-way item used for restoring and wood and metal finishing. Try them for spirit varnishes, lacquers, and every kind of brush.

Beardmore & Co., 4 Percy St, London W1 is *the* place, in case you haven't come across it yet, for brass fittings of every imaginable sort. A good place to browse through in search of shiny bits and bobs for chunky jewellery. But visit them at off-peak times if possible (avoid Saturdays), because otherwise you might have to wait a long time to be served.

John Lewis, Oxford St, London W1 is a shop everyone knows about. But perhaps you didn't know that it remains *the* shop for all those cheap, traditional fabrics like flannel, cheese-cloth, sheeting etc. which can be the devil to track down in provincial department stores and High Streets. They also stock such useful items as beads, embroidery canvas, fringes and bobble trims. To get the best out of a visit to Lewis's allow a morning for browsing systematically through the place. I know designers who haunt Lewis's counters in search of just the right tiny peasant print, or bold gingham or tailoring canvas.

Pontings, Kensington High St, London W8 is a legendary store, a whole chapter of nostalgia to itself situated in a basement below Barker's where you can buy such rarities as green baize. Another designers' haunt.